C000297418

THE MANAGERS GUIDE TO
UNDERSTANDING COMMERCIAL CONTRACT NEGOTIATION

Also available in the *Commercial Contracts for Managers Series*:

- *Understanding Commonly Used Contract Terms*
- *Understanding Confidentiality Agreements*
- *Understanding Effective Contract Evaluation*
- *Understanding Indemnity Clauses*
- *Understanding Tenders*

Commercial Contracts for Managers Series

THE MANAGERS GUIDE TO
UNDERSTANDING
COMMERCIAL
CONTRACT
NEGOTIATION

by

Frank Adoranti

Dip Law (BAB), MBA (UNE), FCIS

**Solicitor and Barrister of the Supreme Court of
New South Wales**

Chartered Secretary

Notary Public

GLOBAL
professional
publishing

First published in Great Britain. 2006
Reprinted 2010

Apart from any fair dealing for the purpose of research or private study, or criticism or review, as permitted under the Copyright, Designs and Patents Act 1988, this publication may only be reproduced, stored or transmitted, in any form or by any means, with the prior permission in writing of the publisher, or in the case of reprographic reproduction in accordance with the terms and licences issued by the Copyright Licensing Agency. Enquiries concerning reproduction outside those terms should be addressed to the publisher. The address is below:

GLOBAL PROFESSIONAL PUBLISHING Limited
Random Acres
Slip Mill Lane
Hawkhurst
Cranbrook
Kent TN18 5AD

GLOBAL PROFESSIONAL PUBLISHING believes that the sources of information upon which the book is based are reliable, and has made every effort to ensure the complete accuracy of the text. However, neither GLOBAL PROFESSIONAL PUBLISHING , the author nor any contributor can accept any legal responsibility whatsoever for consequences that may arise from errors or omissions or any opinion or advice given.

For full details of Global Professional Publishing titles in
Management, Finance and Banking see our website at:
www.gppbooks.com

© Frank Adoranti, 2006

ISBN 978-0-85297-720-0

Cover Designer: Insignia Graphics

Senior Editor: Jessica Perini

Printed in India by Replika Press Pvt. Ltd.

PREFACE

■ ■ ■

Just because you've been signing contracts for years, it doesn't mean you have understood what you've been signing.

One of management's biggest fears is that of an employee exposing the company to the risk of potentially ruinous litigation. It is a fear with genuine foundation.

The cost of litigation is measured in the billions (indeed one estimate is that in the USA alone, the cost is in excess of $200 billion).

A company exposed to litigation suffers the following consequences:

- uncertainty;
- adverse publicity and loss of reputation; and
- expense and drain of management time.

These consequences are the natural enemies of the manager. They undermine the marketplace's perception of the company and can also have adverse effects on a company's share price. This is especially so given the post–Enron/Arthur Andersen climate of business.

During the last six years, I have devoted much time and effort to instilling a culture of litigation prevention in corporations, by the education of managers in fundamental concepts of commercial contracts.

A common question raised by managers at the conclusion of my seminars is: *What book can I read as a ready reference?* Unfortunately, I found no particular book catering to these aspects of corporate legal education. The most common problems expressed to me regarding existing books on the market were that they were:

- **too difficult to read:** the bulk of titles on the market dealing with contracts are scholarly academic works intended for the practising lawyer or law student;

- **not practical:** the less imposing and shorter "guides" are predominantly aimed at law students "cramming" or revising for examinations or oriented to consumer law issues (neighbourhood disputes, family law, wills and personal bankruptcy); and

- **not portable:** none are presented as handy reference guides specifically tailored to managers. They are usually off-putting in their size, length and/or prohibitive expense.

When discussing the concept of a managers' guide to commercial contracts, most of the comments I received from managers can be summarised in the following quotation:

> *Whilst it might not offer the depth of information on a particular topic that a textbook does, a handy guide in your briefcase accessible <u>when you need it</u> is far better than the volumes sitting on a shelf back at your home or office.*

This provided me with the final impetus to fill the need in this area. You hold in your hands the fifth in a series of books catering to this requirement.

The purpose of this book is to provide an explanation of the commercial contract negotiation process. Further, it deals with the translation of the concluded bargain into a written contract.

A number of specific contract issues and clauses relating to negotiation will also be covered.

Along the way, you will find practical tips with examples on some of the traps and pitfalls of commercial contract negotiation.

The aim is to help managers understand such issues to ultimately avoid the aggravation of contract disputes and litigation.

As a safeguard, you should *always* seek qualified advice in specific situations.

When dealing with the law, often, there is no single "right" answer. This series of books will help managers develop the ability to deal with particular aspects of the ambiguities of contracts. They should be of assistance to every manager dealing with commercial contracts and agreements and from sales and business development staff through to the CEO and CFO. The series caters to those in large publicly-listed organisations as well as to smaller businesses.

In writing this series, I have drawn on my 16 years of experience in the law in various countries. I have tried to cut through the mire of theory and "legalese" and distil the essence of a highly technical topic into something easily understandable and digestible for the manager in a hurry.

Where possible, I have used actual examples, taken from situations I have encountered, as illustrations of many of the points made in the book. The names, identities and particular circumstances have, of course, been changed in order to protect the confidentiality of those persons and entities.

I trust you find this series of guides as useful to read as I found them enjoyable to write.

Frank Adoranti

Sydney, March 2006

ACKNOWLEDGMENTS

■ ■ ■

Naturally, a work which is the product of many years of research and development never comes together single-handedly.

Thanks, as always, to my good friend David-Crane, one of the finest property lawyers in the country and also a gentleman (not that the terms are mutually exclusive). I also wish to thank Costas Condoleon for reviewing the manuscript and providing valuable input into improving the quality of the finished product. To Warwick Isherwood, who has — for the second time — subjected himself to an extensive review of one of my manuscripts. Once again, many thanks for sharing the benefit of your considerable expertise and for your exhaustive and most valuable review of the final manuscript. Thanks to Liz Crowhurst, who so richly deserves the many accolades she receives.

Thanks also to Ian Barker QC for his kind permission to reproduce the story of the closed stairwell in Chapter 14. I also extend my gratitude to Francis Wilkins, editor of the *Lawyers Weekly*, for his efforts in securing the author's permission, for the reproduction of the humorous "10 golden rules of negotiation", at the conclusion of the book.

A special and sincere thanks to Justice Michael Kirby, of the High Court of Australia, for his encouragement and kind support.

My thanks to all those who have equipped me with experiences (both positive and not-so-positive) with which to be able to write this book. Some of these experiences have taught me enduring (and sometimes expensive) lessons, which I trust will now be of benefit to you.

We should always be striving to learn, stretch ourselves intellectually and constantly improve — only the incompetent are *always* at their best. A measure of how well we are applying ourselves to the task of self-improvement is the ability to be able to look back and say:

> *I never cease to be amazed at how stupid I was last month.*

To my editor, Jessica Perini; goodness! Is it really five books now? I once again thank you, from the heart, for your enormously valuable contribution. The entire series has gained so much from your experienced eye, your wisdom and ever-cheerful guidance.

To my brother Gino for his friendship.

To my parents; they will always be my treasures and inspiration. My father's example, as a man who achieved and built much from nothing, stands as a model for me to emulate. My mother's total and unconditional love, generosity and warmth never fails to impress.

To Kiara, Gianni and Luca, collectively our greatest source of laughter, fun and good times (as well as an ever-increasing number of grey hairs).

Finally, to my wife Rosalie, for always being the centre of my universe and award-winning mother to our (incredibly cute and good-natured) children.

One has never *really* experienced difficult and complex negotiations until one has tried to do so with one's children ...

ABOUT THE AUTHOR

■ ■ ■

The author has worked in the private practice of law since 1986. Since 1996 he has worked with a number of multinational corporations both in Europe and in the Asia–Pacific region.

As an international corporate lawyer and consultant, he has reviewed thousands of significant commercial agreements and has seen, first hand, the damage that organisations suffer when proper care is not exercised in negotiating and correctly documenting contract terms. He has also conducted and managed hundreds of millions of dollars of litigation in various parts of the world, caused by such lack of care.

For many years, commercial contract negotiations have been a daily (and very often, nightly) part of his life.

He has been involved in a broad range of commercial transactions ranging from the acquisition and sale of international companies to simple confidentiality agreements, and much else in between. He has also assisted organisations with:

- mergers and acquisitions;
- post-merger integrations;
- corporate restructures;
- establishment of tender and bidding processes;
- crisis management planning;
- contract management systems;
- legal audit and legal risk assessments;
- relations with external lawyers;
- planning corporate legal departments;
- compliance programs; and
- in-house training programs and seminars on contracts and other legal issues.

In addition to his qualifications as a lawyer, he has an MBA and is a Fellow of the Institute of Chartered Secretaries and Administrators. He is also a Notary Public.

TABLE OF CONTENTS

■ ■ ■

Chapter 6   During the negotiation

Chapter 7   Negotiating ploys — attempting to gain the upper hand

INTRODUCTION

■ ■ ■

There are many fine books written about negotiation. This book is different in that the primary focus is on *commercial contract negotiations*. It also contains general negotiating principles and information, which are applicable to any other type of negotiation.

In this book, you will not find much of the jargon that exists in "heavyweight" theoretical negotiation books; terms such as:

- *social cognition*
- *decremental deprivation*
- *posterior rationality*

In case you were wondering about the meanings of the above terms — were they to have actually been used in this book, this is how they would have been defined in "plain English":

- **Social cognition**
  The sub-branch of social psychology concerned with understanding why people respond differently to

particular social situations, and how one person's responses to similar events can also differ at various times.

For example, having gone through a gruelling negotiation might spur one person to even greater heights, by looking forward with relish, to the challenge of a similarly gruelling future negotiation; whereas another might shy away from the process, regarding it as too traumatic and taxing to ever wish to repeat.

People process experiences through their individual "filters" of reality. Because these views are unique to a person's personal values, experiences and unique pre-dispositions, each person's interpretation of reality is distinct, causing them to respond differently to events.

- *Decremental deprivation*

This refers to a situation where one's expectations remain constant, whilst the ability to meet those expectations decreases over time.

For example:

— Joe expects to have regular increases in his wage to keep up with cost of living adjustments;

— Whereas, the fortunes of Indecline Co are plummeting. Earnings and profits are falling, so their ability to reward their staff is decreasing.

- *Posterior rationality*

This occurs where one justifies a behaviour or action with information that becomes available only after the event.

For example, Joe Worker, as the Chief Credit Controller, refuses approval for credit to be extended to a particular customer for a seemingly lucrative account. When that customer goes bankrupt several months later, Joe says, using posterior rationality:

That's why I didn't grant them the extra credit.

What you *will* find in this book is a wealth of practical and useful information you can readily identify and immediately apply in your next negotiation. Some of the anecdotes may strike a reminiscent chord within you. In any event, the aim is for this manual to be a useful learning tool, detailing the relevant principles and illustrating their application, in a commercial context.

I have endeavoured to be as light as possible on the theory and as heavy as possible on the practical side.

We will commence by canvassing the fundamentals of commercial contract negotiation such as the characteristics of a good negotiator, together with crucial issues such as the impact of time, bargaining power and authority on negotiations. Next, we will examine the negotiating mindset and its importance. We will also consider the critical issue of maintaining personal credibility.

Just as a golf instructor will always go back to the very basics of your golf swing, we will go back to the fundamentals of negotiation, which constitute an important basis for revision and reminder.

We will look at how different cultures will influence and require you to modify your behaviour and conduct, to maximise the benefits flowing to you. You will also learn to be sensitive to the subtle cultural differences.

Competitive situations can produce different negotiating perspectives. We will look at the different influences in competitive negotiation situations, such as auctions.

The need to carefully plan negotiations and determine clear objectives is highlighted. These objectives will influence the selection of a single negotiating strategy or mixture of strategies. Naturally, these must be sufficiently flexible so as to be able to evolve and develop, to ensure they are appropriate to the flow of the negotiation. We will also examine the difference between commercial decisions and legal issues.

The impact and effect of differing negotiating styles will be covered, to enable you to determine which approach will be the most appropriate for your given situation. Sometimes, you will realise that you can "attract more flies with honey than with vinegar". Other times, the use of "vinegar" may be the preferred (or, indeed, the only available) approach.

The chapters on common negotiating ploys and common myths provide you with some useful tips to help you "survive" the negotiation process and to the final transition to a written contract. You may recognise some of these tricks. They may have either been used by you or against you. The rationale for their presentation is to help you develop an awareness of when they are being used against you — so that you can formulate appropriate defence strategies and thereby avoid falling for any tricks or sharp practices.

You will learn why it is often best (and sometimes legally necessary) to have agreements in writing. Also some legal rules of contract interpretation will be canvassed, as you will need to bear these in mind when recording details, for later incorporation into a contract document.

As the book is dedicated to commercial contract negotiations, it will help you translate the negotiation process into a clear and unambiguous contract document.

The process of moving from the negotiation table to contract will be examined and some of the potential pitfalls will be uncovered for the reader.

Issues surrounding the actual drafting of contract documents, such as who draws the documents, the treatment of drafts and the process of "marking-up" drafts, will (among other issues) be considered. We will also examine the negotiation of common (and vitally important) specific types of contracts and clauses such as confidentiality agreements. The main recurring negotiating points will be illustrated, together with some details on the trend towards demanding exclusivity on a deal and when it is appropriate to require a break-fee.

Commonly occurring contract drafting pitfalls — relevant to a commercial negotiation — will then be covered. A failure to understand such pitfalls can severely dilute or diminish the value of the time and effort invested in the negotiation process. In extreme cases, it could even render the entire negotiation process a waste of time. Paying attention to these aspects *during* the negotiation process (rather than as an afterthought) is equivalent to the proverbial "ounce of prevention" being worth "a pound of cure". You will gain an understanding of some of the common expressions or practices that one should best avoid.

We will then turn to an examination of some relevant rules of contract interpretation. These will assist you in developing an awareness of their impact at the *front end* of the transaction, when you still retain the ability to influence changes (by negotiation) in a draft contract. Once the document is executed and the parties are arguing over it, an awareness of these rules will not serve you as well.

Some of the more common negotiated legal issues are also covered, such as joint and several liability provisions and indemnity clauses. These are powerful devices and have wide and far-reaching effects. You will learn when they are appropriate and when not.

As you read further, you will see references to other titles in the *Commercial Contracts for Managers Series*. These flow onto topics that are closely interrelated, and necessary to achieve an understanding of commercial contracts and of the commercial contract issues that are most commonly encountered in business.

Some of the principles will not be new to you, but should be a useful reminder or refresher. The case studies are designed to demonstrate the application of some of the principles in a practical way. The case studies also contain some practical hints and tips.

I trust you will find the material assembled within this book to be useful and applicable in your everyday business.

Chapter 1

FOUNDATION

■ ■ ■

Negotiation is one of the most fundamental skills in business. For those fed on a constant diet of the evening news, the word "negotiation" produces connotations of trade union wage demands or diplomatic peace talks. However, a negotiation can be about something as mundane as whose turn it is to clean up, which programme the family watches on TV, or who gets the keys to the family car for the evening.

It is probably the single most used skill in business and in life generally; whether we are trying to influence a superior or subordinate at work, customer or supplier, or even a spouse, child or parent at home.

Negotiation is not litigation nor is it war; it is *not* about obtaining a total victory on all points.

Tactics such as "hardball" and "scorched earth" methods, when consistently and indiscriminately applied in a given situation, achieve little in the long run. Notice that I say *consistently* applied. There will be situations when such approaches may be called for or become necessary. To retain their maximum effectiveness, they should be resorted to sparingly.

Total victory contracts tend to be short-lived for a number of reasons; the bankruptcy of the party "squeezed" on the deal can be one of those reasons.

The exception is the situation where a large company (with adequate capacity) takes on a deal as a known loss-leader. This might be to enter into a new area of business or to secure a contract with a particular strategic value or significance.

Otherwise, such "one way" deals merely encourage the party on the "bad" end of the deal to find ways of cutting corners and quality, in an attempt to make the contract profitable. If there is enough money involved and the other party feels wronged, the incentive to search for the legal "loophole" or even to fight (even if only "for the principle"), can be a highly destructive force.

This is not the recipe for a happy long-term relationship.

Equally, a failure to detect gambit or ploy, used to secure an unfair advantage against you in a negotiation, can be a costly mistake with a lasting impact — often for many years during the life of a contract.

> ### Golden Rule
>
> In negotiation, *preventative* measures and safeguards are the best tools available.
>
> Once you have been outmanoeuvred into accepting an unduly onerous contract, it may be too late to renegotiate, at least without risk to your personal reputation.
>
> You cannot "unring" the proverbial bell.

Neither directors nor managers wish to be exposed to potential personal liability or ridicule for being out-negotiated, and committing their company to a contract that did not maximise the company's benefit. Worse still would be the case where credibility and reputations of both the organisation and the persons involved were adversely affected or even irreparably damaged.

These factors combine to make a fundamental understanding of commercial contract negotiations more relevant than ever.

Commercial contract negotiation is an interesting mixture of both negotiating skill and legal flair. There are many opportunities to be creative in the quest to achieve a solution acceptable to two different parties, with (usually) competing interests. It is indeed greatly satisfying to help develop a mutually acceptable resolution to what was originally a seemingly insurmountable negotiating obstacle.

Chapter 2

CHARACTERISTICS OF A GOOD NEGOTIATOR

■ ■ ■

To become an accomplished negotiator you need to:

- have well-developed communication skills;
- be empathetic;
- be creative;
- approach the negotiation with an open frame of mind;
- be a good motivator;
- be credible;
- be a strong person; and
- have good people skills.

These characteristics are not to be considered in isolation. They are all intertwined, and when combined, produce an accomplished negotiator.

Naturally, as we are describing humans, with all their foibles and differences, you will find that different people have differing measures of each trait. This mixture alone, is sufficient to produce varying outcomes, even though they may arise from a similar set of circumstances.

■ ■ ■

Good communicator

Communicating does not only mean speaking or writing. It is the interaction of the speaking, writing and listening functions.

Listening does not simply consist of acknowledging what the other side is trying to say. It is the skill of being able to genuinely appreciate and understand what it is the other party wants and to assess this in relation to your own objectives.

Assuming that a negotiated bargain is one acceptable to all sides, it follows that all good thinking in a negotiation arises from listening and understanding the relevant issues from all sides.

Clarity in all communication, whether written or oral, saves time and potential antagonism in a negotiation, by avoiding misunderstandings such as:

*When you said a **substantial** order, I thought you meant at least 1000 units, not the 100 units that you had in mind!*

An important part of being a good communicator and listener is to ensure that points are agreed to unambiguously and clearly, in order to ensure that the negotiations over such points do not need to be, effectively, reopened.

One way to achieve this is to accurately record the progress of the negotiations over those points, with any necessary qualifications required by one party or the other. Also, such notes will make it significantly easier to brief your lawyer when it comes time to:

- finally draw the contract; or

- verify a draft contract produced by the other side's lawyers.

■ ■ ■

Empathy

Empathy is the ability to experience the feelings or ideas of another person. This helps not only to establish a negotiating rapport but also gives you the ability to genuinely place yourself in the position of the other party.

This trait can enable you to think more laterally and creatively and to perhaps see a different solution, that might not have been otherwise apparent to the self-interested negotiator.

■ ■ ■

Creativity

Creativity requires solution-oriented thinking. Every move must be considered with the end solution in mind; considering also that there might be more than one solution to a problem and that an alternative solution might prove to have less unwanted consequences for one of the parties and therefore, be more suitable to everyone.

Being creative involves a certain element of flexibility. The recognition of the evolutionary process of a negotiation is critical. To enter a negotiation with a rigid plan and an iron will to adhere to it, regardless of the flow of proceedings, is not the hallmark of an able negotiator.

The element of creativity can also involve the ability to restate a problem in a slightly different way. This can trigger an examination of the issues from different angles. Thus, issues not previously considered can be uncovered, or a proposed solution to a problem can be refined.

Case study: splitting the orange

One recalls the classic example of the two children, **Gianni** and **Luca**, fighting over an orange. Each of them asserted, with equal vigour, their desire to have that last remaining orange.

To quickly settle the dispute, their well-meaning **father** suggested the simple *split it down the middle* solution of cutting the orange into two halves and giving each of the children one half.

However, the wise **grandfather** took the step of sitting down with each of the children and asking each of them their reason for wanting the orange.

As it turned out, **Gianni** wanted to squeeze the orange to make orange juice, whereas **Luca** wanted to use the peel to incorporate it into a recipe.

Even though both children wanted the orange, they each had different reasons for wanting it.

The well-meaning **father's** knee-jerk response to split the orange 50/50 between the children, would have left them both unsatisfied.

Such a compromise would have effectively produced a lose–lose situation for the children, whereas the wise **grandfather's** more creative solution produced a win–win situation, giving each of them 100% of what they originally wanted.

■ ■ ■

Strength

There is indeed strength in gentleness.

Being strong has nothing to do with being antagonistic or stubborn. There is a saying among trial lawyers that *cross-examination is not simply examining crossly*. One can be strong by being firm. That does not equate to being overbearing or angry when making or emphasising a point. It is the ones who shout the most or *attempt* to look the strongest, who are in reality, among the weakest.

Confidence is part of strength, but not *over-confidence*, which can easily be interpreted as arrogance. The best source of confidence is achieved through:

- thorough preparation;
- knowledge and familiarity of the issues; and
- knowledge of the motivating factors of the other side.

Strength is a necessary trait in a negotiation when a stand needs to be taken; either on a particular issue or point, or even in relation to excessive amounts of abysmal conduct by the other side. A certain amount of tenacity is also an advantage.

■ ■ ■

People skills

The ability to get along and be likeable is important. Notice that being liked does not mean being sycophantic or craving to be liked at any cost. It refers to the genuine appreciation that both sides are attempting to secure a workable arrangement. People skills help one to be attuned and responsive to the objectives of the other side. This does not mean that you always accommodate the other side's wishes. It means that you are able to recognise, in a co-operative and sensible way, a situation where a request simply cannot be acceded to or even that a deal cannot be reached by the parties.

Also, the ability to read and understand the non-verbal signals in a negotiation is critical. Just ask any poker player.

Cultural issues become highly relevant and are intertwined in any discussion of people skills. See also the section on **Negotiating cultures** in Chapter 4.

This is where careful preparation prior to the negotiation and proper intelligence gathering can help you better read, understand and interact with your negotiating counterpart. Otherwise, you might simply embarrass yourself and others — which may negatively impact the pursuit of your negotiating objectives.

The definition of people skills extends to include the ability to read and judge an overall situation, in order to know when to keep pushing on a particular issue and when not to do so.

One must also be attuned to those who remain passive and voice no opinion during a negotiation, then later refuse, lose, or endlessly amend contracts. This might be simply because they are incapable of saying "no" in person, but will use every other method thereafter to stall or kill a project or deal.

Possessing a modicum of people skills will also help you to recognise when the people with whom you are negotiating do not have people skills.

For example, when persons during a negotiation may be conducting themselves in a manner that is totally insensitive or indifferent to the interests and objectives of the other side; such indifference can stifle any meaningful dialogue and negotiating creativity that a solutions-oriented negotiation can often produce. People skills can help you to extract the correct information from them, to help them say what they have to say.

People skills can also teach you to be aware of those who see any competitive situation (such as a negotiation) as requiring them to adopt an attitude of "kill or be killed", and can help you defuse and neutralise such negative behavioural patterns.

■■■

Frame of mind

Seeking total victory

To restate an earlier point, negotiation is not litigation, nor is it a war; it is not about obtaining a total victory on all points. Obtaining total victory over a party only generates animosity, rather than the goodwill necessary to sustain a long-term commercial relationship. No "blood" needs to be spilled in a successful and productive negotiation.

Winning good business

Anyone can shake hands on a deal. The true test is whether the parties actually end up obtaining the benefits they bargained for when the deal was struck.

That is why incentives to sales people should, ideally, not be based on just "winning the business". They should be geared towards winning *good* business. Often, such an assessment cannot be made for years after a deal has been secured.

Spirit of co-operation

Parties usually come to a negotiating table to strike a deal that is in each of their interests. The most appropriate frame of mind for the parties to adopt is one of co-operation rather than an adversarial approach, with its attendant hostilities. If the parties can't get on for a few hours or days at the negotiation table, how on earth can they possibly co-exist peacefully in a long-term commercial relationship?

Looking for ulterior motives — the hidden agenda

Some parties might enter into a commercial negotiation with no intention of reaching a concluded bargain. They may have another interest in spoiling the process to either help "chew up" time or to divert the other party from a competitor in a situation where multiple-parties may be negotiating contemporaneously.

Obviously, your intelligence-gathering and qualifying processes are important to enable you to detect such "sharp" practices.

One frequently used tactic to chew-up time is the constant and continual over-use of the following:

We'll take your comments on board.

OR

We'll deal with this issue later.

OR

We don't have that information available; we'll get back to you on that.

Case study: how to negotiate when you don't really want to...

There are some situations, particularly in diplomatic negotiations, where one party has no intention of actually attempting a genuine negotiation over an issue. In such an event, a party can put on a "front" to demonstrate its good faith.

Teams of negotiators enter into hard-fought negotiations over such spurious matters as the selection and location of the venue, or the size, height and orientation of the tables. Then, the number, and identity of the participants becomes an "issue". The agenda to be followed and the order of the items can also be fodder for contrived and trivial argument. All of this can often take days to resolve, rather than dealing with the real issues.

If taken to extremes (which it sometimes is), this process either wears down the other side or causes the negotiations to completely derail. This, of course, represents the desired outcome for the party wishing to "spoil" the negotiation and "run down the clock".

Then the "spoiling" party can't be accused of being so intractable as to refuse to even participate in the process. This is often accompanied by the appropriate posturing that the "spoiling" party genuinely desired a negotiated solution but had "a number of" serious and valid concerns to guarantee the "fairness" of the process.

It is more face-saving for them to say that the talks simply "broke down", were "adjourned" or "suspended indefinitely" — perhaps to be rescheduled to another time and place.

More often than not, this is where the entire sorry process ends.

■ ■ ■

Negotiating skill

Like driving a car, it is impossible to learn negotiation from a book or classroom, alone. If the clock isn't ticking against you, as it is in a real negotiation, there is nothing at stake, your reputation is not on the line. The fears and desires that drive negotiations towards agreements are not present.

As the Mexican proverb says:

Talking about bulls is not the same as facing them in the ring.

Negotiation is best learned by actually negotiating and applying the principles you have learned. Naturally, you should first learn the fundamental principles, to avoid making a total fool of yourself.

What takes longer to learn and can only be accumulated by experience is the good sense to assess a situation and make certain judgment calls with confidence. For example, experience teaches you to *differentiate opinions and feelings from objective facts.*

Consider statements most of us have heard, at one time or another, during the course of a negotiation such as:

They would never agree to your proposal.

OR

I don't think we can pay that much.

OR

We haven't budgeted for that.

These statements are *subjective* expressions of opinions or feelings. They are not statements of fact. The difference is subtle. Experience helps you to discern and detect them when you hear them.

Experience also teaches you to rank your main points prior to the negotiation. Your efforts are then focused on those. Once you achieve them, you can concentrate on finding ways to help the other party achieve their objectives.

Inexperienced negotiators tend to give all of their points equal weight and regard each one as a battle to win. They do not know when to concede and move on from a non-material point.

■ ■ ■

Being a good motivator

Looking for and finding ways of motivating the other side can enhance your ability to persuade them. Remember that the things that motivate us may not necessarily have the same effect upon others. One should never assume that what matters to us matters to anyone else.

Remember:

One man's food is another man's poison.

OR

One man's trash is another man's treasure.

This means you have to be attuned to the wants and needs of the other side and constantly look for ways to press these "buttons". In this way, you will generate the appropriate level of interest for your point of view.

Case study: the right incentive

A violent cyclone was rapidly approaching Smallville. Police were frantically attempting to evacuate residents from their homes.

They conducted a door-knock of the homes of people who had refused to heed previous calls to leave. The continued urging of the police was of little use, as the more stubborn residents thought they could "batten down the hatches" and "ride out" the storm.

Realising that time was running against them, the police changed their methods. They decided to try a different and ultimately more persuasive approach — they offered a new kind of incentive.

The police simply asked the residents who had decided to remain to provide a saliva swab for a DNA sample — in order to facilitate the identification of their bodies, after the storm.

Responding to the new message, the remaining residents scrambled to their cars sooner than the police could move out of their way!

It takes a little creative thinking to find the right "buttons to push" in order to motivate and inspire people to action.

■■■

Credibility

Credibility is an important tool to have at your disposal in any negotiation. It is also highly portable, and knowledge thereof (or, more particularly, of the absence thereof) usually precedes your arrival at any negotiation.

It always pays to remember that this negotiation is not your first and will also not be your last. You need to ensure that you emerge from each negotiation with your credibility intact. It will be extremely rare for there to be a negotiation where you should willingly risk losing it. You will, in all likelihood, need it again. It is also important to protect the credibility of your organisation.

To help maintain your credibility, you need to be mindful of:

- **Making consistently rash claims or demands.**

  Notice the use of the word "consistently" in the above statement.

  There will be situations when making a rash or exaggerated claim, statement or demand may be appropriate or necessary.

  To retain the maximum effectiveness of such tactics and your, all-important credibility, it should be done frugally. *Any* tactic, when overused, loses its effect.

- **Be acutely aware of making absolute statements in a negotiation.**

  For example, if you have made an offer and accompany it with a statement such as: "This is my final offer."

  After having made such a statement, you are not in a position to then move from your position, *under any circumstances*. To do so, for any reason, is a real risk to your credibility.

This is why you should exercise great care in making absolute statements of any kind in a negotiation. If you are instructed to do so by your superiors, you should make it abundantly clear to them that there is no room for a change of heart thereafter, in order to maintain the credibility of both the organisation and of yourself.

You want to be known as a person whose word means something.

- **Not following through with a promise or threat.**

  If you have threatened to walk away from the negotiation over a deal-breaker, you must be prepared do so.

  You should avoid a situation requiring you to place your credibility on the line. However, if you have placed your credibility on the line during a negotiation and there has been a change of heart at the top and where a return to the negotiation would damage your personal credibility, you should ensure that someone else (preferably somebody placed further up the organisational ladder) returns to announce the sudden turnaround.

  To emphasise an earlier point, threats and promises should be made sparingly — so that when they are made, your reputation will cause them to be regarded as "bankable" by the recipient.

- **Do not bluff.**

  If you do and are caught out, the other side will assume you are bluffing whenever you take a hard line. Don't forget "the boy who cried wolf".

Besides killing your credibility, this will also have the effect of prolonging the negotiation. This is because the other side will then wish to probe each remaining issue to its depths, to be satisfied that you are not also bluffing on those issues.

If you do threaten to leave the negotiation, be sure you are ready to do so, especially when you may be invited by your opponents to carry out your threat. If you don't, you will have lost your credibility and will be in real trouble.

It is a genuine pleasure (though not easy, by any means) doing business with people who have a reputation for credibility.

Chapter 3

FACTORS AFFECTING NEGOTIATION

■ ■ ■

Time pressures

Most negotiations have some element of time-sensitivity to them. Being away from your home city, for example, can create its own time pressures. See more in the section **Logistics — your place or mine?**

One rule during any negotiation is not to disclose any time pressure that you might be under. Announcing during a negotiation that:

I have a flight to catch at 5 pm

will almost certainly guarantee that progress will be slowed and that "unforeseen" issues will emerge.

You will then be under additional pressure of having to either decide to return home empty handed, or to accept something considerably less than you might have accepted otherwise.

Knowledge of another's time pressures can give you the edge. For example, if you know of a production schedule the other side might have, this might provide you with some bargaining power.

One way to maintain momentum or accelerate negotiations, is to put pressure on the other side to act by imposing deadlines for certain steps. For example:

I will need your answer by 9 am tomorrow

OR

The board is meeting at 10.30 am on Wednesday

OR

If I don't have your commitment by Monday, at close of business, I will have to put it back onto the market

These statements all have the effect of creating pressure by compressing the decision-making timeframe. Time is a precious commodity in a negotiation. Any action that shortens that time — by its very nature — applies some kind of pressure upon the other.

Note that deadlines require precision to be effective.

If you require someone to provide you with a response "by 9 am Tuesday", you must specifically say so. Otherwise, to simply require a response by "Tuesday" could easily mean "by 11.59 pm Tuesday" to someone else.

Deadlines don't just happen, they are created. Some might be artificial and meaningless, some are not. Being able to differentiate between those two kinds of deadlines, will prevent the shift in bargaining power against you. The ability to discern between the two is born of experience — reading the people and the signs. Are the actions of the other side consistent with the stated deadlines? Have they previously stated deadlines that have been easily extended or shifted?

Be aware that most deadlines are not the life and death issues they are made to seem. Many are more flexible than you might initially imagine.

Naturally, one way to counter any deadline imposed upon you is to ask for the reason behind the deadline. Probing is the key.

Why do I need to get back to you by tomorrow? Why the rush?

OR

> *Surely the board can delegate its authority for a decision to be made if it can't happen before Wednesday?*

OR

> *If you do not already have a committed buyer such as us ready to proceed, what difference will an extra day make when we are this close to closing the deal? You're surely not going to discard us after all the progress we have made?*

When confronted by any deadline put to you, consider it in the context of some of these questions:

- *What will **really** happen if this passes?*
- *How serious will the consequences be?*
- *Will there, in fact, be any **real** consequences?*
- *Are they bluffing?*
- *Would they **really** walk away?*

Just remember that assessments such as these are subjective and that even the best negotiators can size up a situation incorrectly. This is the inherent risk involved in making judgment calls about a situation. Typically, good judgment comes with experience.

One further point to remember about time is that the greater the investment of time by a party, the harder it then becomes for them to walk away empty-handed, with nothing to show for the days/weeks/months of effort. The longer you can keep them at the table, the more likely it is that you can do a deal.

The message is certainly not to ignore deadlines, but to question them and analyse them, to determine their level of truth and importance.

■ ■ ■

Auction situations

In any mergers and acquisition (M&A) situation — such as the purchase or sale of a business, or even a takeover situation — the introduction of competitive tension, the introduction of the heightened competitive tension of the auction situation, tends to drive prices skyward. It is one of the tools of trade that investment bankers may use to maximise the return on sale to a vendor client.

In such a situation, when you make or receive an offer, carefully consider those other parties who may also be interested — whilst also considering those who should be interested but are not. Do they know something that you do not?

Your objective as an executive is to secure the best price and the best terms:

- as a vendor, to maximise your sale price and minimise your residual liability (after the conclusion of the sale process); and

- as a purchaser to minimise your investment in the purchase price and to maximise your recourse upon the vendor (after the sale) in the event of any breach of warranty or condition.

Golden Rule

The introduction of competitive tension into auction-like situations, can significantly increase prices achieved.

This generally applies regardless of the dollar value of the object sold — whether it is a substantial company being sold through a prestigious investment-banking house, or whether it is a collectible figurine being sold on an auction website.

It is a product of human nature — that we are more likely to want something if we know that someone else wants it too.

Therefore, a buyer must always be concerned to ensure that it does not pay too much for the company it intends to purchase.

Remember that the competitive tension that exists between buyers can be used to maximum effect by sellers to, not only, secure the best price, but to also extract from buyers concessions and terms more favourable to the seller.

Golden Nugget

M&A — Are you getting value?

As a buyer, it is usually quite a challenge to extract value from an M&A transaction. Research suggests that as many as 60% of mergers and acquisitions are unsuccessful from the acquirer's point of view.

Often, this occurs because, in a competitive auction, there is a tendency for the highest bidder to typically pay a premium to win the auction.

Such a premium can nullify (or at least greatly mitigate) any expected value that the acquisition was ever going to generate. In extreme cases, the premium can sometimes be greater than the expected benefits of the deal, for some years. This can mean that a number of years might elapse before the acquirer can begin to count on a return on the investment.

Where the acquisition takes place for a particular strategic reason (such as the initiation of, or expansion of, a core business in a particular territory), the acquirer will have already planned for such a premium to be paid and will have budgeted for it when projecting its future return on investment (ROI).

Many of us have heard stories of "dummy" bidders at residential housing auctions — a method used to artificially inflate the purchase price of a home. Such practices have been known to extend to situations where a business or company is being sold.

Consider a situation where an intermediary, such as an investment bank, is attempting to sell a particular company for a client. In the event that there might be only one interested buyer, there will be a tendency to do whatever possible (within the bounds of ethical and proper conduct) to mask that fact, so that the purchaser is allowed to think that another (or others) may also be interested.

In the event that the purchaser gets wind of the fact that it is the "only buyer in town", the shift in negotiating power is marked.

That is why intelligence gathering and careful research of the situation are important in such competitive situations. The stakes can be quite high. In a major M&A transaction, the difference can be measured in tens of millions of dollars.

Golden Rule

When considering the competitive tensions in a particular situation, give careful thought to whether such competitive tensions are *real* or *manufactured for the other party's benefit*.

■ ■ ■

Authority

Do the persons you are about to negotiate with have sufficient authority to be able to consummate the deal, if an agreement is reached?

On one hand, many experienced negotiators would prefer **not** have all decision-makers present at the negotiating table. They will wish to retain a higher authority (outside the negotiation) to have to consult on the pivotal issues to the deal. The ability to go away and regroup can often be a significant tactical advantage, when the pressure is being applied.

A tactic, sometimes used in some Asian cultures, is to ensure that the negotiation or discussion team is comprised of relatively junior members of the organisation (usually with impressive sounding titles). This means that any "concluded" deal points may be effectively re-opened for negotiation when you are informed that the person with whom you had "agreed" to a particular point *had no authority to discuss or agree this point with you.* See **Cultural differences in practice** in **Chapter 4** for further discussion on this topic.

The higher authority might usually be the CEO. Some might think that a CEO cannot use the higher authority ploy. This of course is incorrect; the CEO can always use his or her board of directors, shareholders or the parent company as the higher authorities, when necessary.

On the other hand, experienced negotiators will want to be certain that all of the decision-makers are present at the negotiation (or, at least, easily contactable to secure their appropriate consent) or that those present have the necessary authority to strike a deal if an agreement is reached.

This is usually done in two steps:

1) By announcing, ahead of the negotiation meeting, the intention to have all decision-makers on both sides present and securing the other side's agreement to the proposition.

2) At the meeting, the first order of business, before any negotiations commence, is confirmation of the fact that all decision-makers with authority are present. In the absence of an express confirmation of full authority, some will insist on adjourning the meeting until such time that all of such persons can be present. They may also wish to castigate the other side for not complying with their agreement to do so.

The paragraphs above do not, of course, apply to initial, preliminary or exploratory meetings, where the parties are trying to ascertain whether a deal would be feasible, possible or desirable.

■■■

Decisions for a manager or a lawyer?

Issues that require evaluation can either be legal or commercial. This is an important distinction.

This distinction divides issues that need to be dealt with by lawyers and those that are commercial terms requiring decisions to be made by managers. For example, if a manager wishes to make a price concession in a contract negotiation — assuming the manager can still "make the numbers" — the issue should have nothing to do with the lawyers and should remain the responsibility of the manager or their superior.

By the same token, managers should not seek to absolve themselves from all decision-making responsibility or the consequences thereof by having lawyers sign off on everything; even on issues that are not strictly legal ones.

A deal can be placed in jeopardy (or even be lost) when commercial people abdicate total responsibility to their lawyers or, worse still, where an overzealous lawyer decides they know what is right for the company and will therefore take decisions on commercial matters for the client.

Of course, to achieve a harmonious balance, much depends upon the ability of:

- the lawyer to know which decisions are properly commercial ones for the client to ultimately make; and

- the manager to properly brief the lawyer and to realise where an overzealous lawyer might be overstepping the boundaries.

Fortunately, many lawyers will recognise a situation where a manager has not defined proper parameters within which that lawyer must act. Most lawyers will advise their client when a decision is a commercial matter for the manager to decide.

If a manager's brief to a lawyer is for the company to be *absolutely protected*, the only way to achieve such a state of protection is for the lawyer to advise the client not to proceed with the deal. This is because any deal involves risk.

If a manager ever gave an over-zealous lawyer a carte blanche brief, to exercise total control over a transaction, there is every possibility that the deal could fall apart and the commercial relationship between the contract parties be adversely affected. One example of this occurs where an overprotective lawyer (inflexibly) demands the inclusion of the most onerous warranties into a contract.

Case study: XYZ Publishing

Commercial decision or legal decision?

Let us consider some common parameters within which line managers can acceptably deal.

For example, consider the situation of a book publishing company. An acquisitions editor may only have the authority to vary certain terms of a publishing contract offered to an author.

Let us look at four separate situations that might confront the typical acquisitions editor of a major publisher, in a negotiation over a book contract. The author:

1) wants to hold all copyright in the work;

2) has requested the royalty payable on book sales be increased from 10% to 15%;

3) wants 10 extra free copies of the book;

4) wants a research grant of up to $1000; and

5) declines to grant the publisher an indemnity in respect of the originality of the work.

Of the five situations listed, which are those that are effectively commercial decisions likely to only have a budgetary ($) impact alone and not affect the publisher's legal position?

Situations 2), 3) and 4) would appear to be commercial decisions that can be safely made by the relevant line manager concerned. These situations do not require legal input. For example, giving an author 10 extra free books does not legally prejudice the publisher. It is simply a question of dollars.

Whereas, the question of copyright in situation 1) is an intellectual property issue. The indemnity question in situation 5) is definitely a legal issue. These and other similar contract variations should, as a matter of prudence, be scrutinised by the legal department.

Ideally, the lawyer should be involved in the drafting of the wording in all five scenarios of the case study, in order to ensure the wording accurately reflects the agreement reached.

Taking matters one step further, *everything* is ultimately a commercial decision — although not always for a line manager to decide upon. When we become involved in decisions of corporate policy, we must then go to the organisation's apex for the final decision to be made.

In the instance of the case study above, the publisher's CEO might have a good reason to make a call against legal advice in relation to the indemnity clause. Of course, it is the lawyer's task to ensure that management have the full facts and are cognisant of the risks involved.

Once the lawyer has performed that task, the ultimate decision (as well as the responsibility for it) will be taken by the relevant manager.

It is not good practice for a manager to allow lawyers to lead the entire negotiation. Where portions of the discussions are centred solely on legal issues, it is, naturally appropriate to do so. If the lawyer is trusted, one might allow them to use their initiative on relevant legal issues and perhaps use them in a good cop/bad cop role on difficult issues (see the section on **Good cop/bad cop** in Chapter 7 to see how this can be done). However, the lawyer should not be the one calling all of the shots in a commercial negotiation.

It can indeed be despairing to be involved in a negotiation where a manager will simply defer to their lawyers on everything.

Golden Rule

The key is to ensure that you *identify* and *understand* the risks, often by taking proper advice.

> Only then, are you are in a position to make a *commercial judgment* on whether to accept or reject the risk, based on its likely return.

■■■

Bargaining power

Parties may not be of equal bargaining strength. However, you should not think that your counterpart has all the power; even in a situation where you might feel desperate.

Both parties at the table want or need something. Otherwise, they wouldn't be there.

In such a situation, it helps to ask yourself the question:

Why are they negotiating with me?

Bargaining strength is not a static concept. It is continually shifting during the course of a negotiation. Everything that is said and done by the parties during a negotiation produces a subtle shift in the dynamic. Everything that you say or do during a negotiation either helps or hinders your cause in some way. Of course, some things might have an imperceptible impact, whilst others have a more dramatic impact. Make no mistake, though, *everything* that is said and done counts in some way.

Two of the more tangible primary forces that operate to bring about a shift in bargaining power are:

- **Time**

  The party under the greatest time pressure to do a deal tends to "crack" first and give in.

  For example, if the other side learns of the fact that you need to announce the deal at your company's annual general meeting in few days, it has an enhanced ability to "squeeze" you to extract greater concessions than it otherwise could have done, were it not for the time pressure you were under.

  Good negotiators will sense this and s-l-o-w down the progress of matters.

- **Desperation (who wants it more?)**

  To restate a proposition made earlier, the party that is prepared to walk away tends to achieve the best deal.

  Again, desperation is something a good negotiator will sense from the words, actions and demeanour of the parties. When they sense desperation, astute negotiators will increase their demands, even to the point of exaggeration. A negotiator will escalate to demands, that in normal circumstances, might be regarded as outrageous — where there is equal bargaining power between the parties. This is especially so where demands escalating in magnitude are being easily acceded to by the other side. The negotiator will want to probe the limits of how far the other side can be pushed.

Alternatively, if desperation is sensed, without going through such an escalation process, an astute negotiator might simply make an outrageous demand to "test the waters" and better ascertain the extent of the other party's desperation. Depending upon the response received to such outrageous demands, the astute negotiator is better able to ascertain the "malleability" of his or her negotiating opponent.

■ ■ ■

Logistics — your place or mine?

The location of the negotiations can be of importance. The home turf advantage affords you facilities and support that might give you control of the drafting. See the section **Who draws the contracts?** in Chapter 10 for more about this advantage.

Control over the agenda of the meeting might sometimes come with the home turf advantage. Such control over a negotiation or meeting agenda can sometimes also give you the edge in controlling what is discussed and what finally goes into the written agreement.

There will be occasions on which the home turf advantage might carry very little significance, especially if the party with whom you are negotiating is in the same city.

However, once you leave your city or country, then the factors of time, cost and being away may work against you. Travel budgets, accommodation budgets and people's tolerance for being away from home are not unlimited. You may be tempted to make concessions you may not otherwise have made.

Some may be tempted to use the home turf advantage to implement the age-old psychological power plays of strategic seating arrangements or even, in extreme cases, making the visitors' seating lower than their own. This may even extend to providing the visitors with a cramped and window-less office area, for use as a private meeting room.

Experienced negotiators will avoid such clichés "like the plague" (as perhaps I should have, in that sentence). These are cheap and transparent ways of trying to obtain an advantage.

Nowadays, with negotiators becoming more sophisticated, the use of such tactics tends to create amusement in the people they are used against, or in extreme cases may even produce a hostile backlash and bring about an early (and inconclusive) end to the negotiation.

Jurisdiction

Logic might suggest that this be one of the *first* items to be dealt with on a contract drafting agenda. However, in practice it is often one of the *last*, or more incidental issues to be determined.

However, its importance should not be discounted — as it can have an enormous impact on the cost of any subsequent litigation. Litigation can be an expensive proposition when it occurs domestically. The situation worsens when you need to fly managers and staff abroad for the process. You may even have to employ two sets of lawyers (one set domestically and one abroad).

When drafting the actual contract, the parties will need to agree upon the law of a particular place governing the interpretation of the contract document.

The contract will also need to specify the applicable jurisdiction; that is, which courts (of a particular state or country) are empowered to hear and adjudicate upon any disputes arising from the contract. For example, such a statement will specifically declare the contract to be governed by and interpreted under the laws of New South Wales (or the laws of Singapore, the State of Delaware USA — as examples) with the courts of that state having jurisdiction.

The party with the conduct of the drafting of the contract will tend to choose its own local law and jurisdiction, where possible.

The debate over jurisdiction usually centres around the location of the parties and, more particularly, the location of the subject matter of the contract.

In the case of the performance of a singular service in a particular location, the task of determining an appropriate jurisdiction can be relatively easy.

However, the task becomes more complicated if, for example, a Swiss firm (**"Swissco"**) is performing a service (or supplying goods) to subsidiaries — located in different countries throughout Asia — of a British parent company (**"Britco"**). How do we best choose the appropriate jurisdiction when negotiating the terms of the Master Supply Agreement between **Swissco** and **Britco**? Probably by negotiation between the lawyers. If **Britco** (the purchaser of the services) is in a stronger bargaining position, it may have the advantage of securing the applicable law and jurisdiction as its own — in such case, **Swissco** might wish the jurisdiction to be best left as "non-exclusive".

For a more detailed examination of jurisdiction clauses and an explanation of the differences between exclusive and non-exclusive jurisdiction, you should consult *Understanding Commonly Used Contract Terms: Boilerplate Clauses*, the fourth volume in the *Commercial Contracts for Managers Series*.

■ ■ ■

Qualifying the other party

A corollary of the authority rule is to ensure that you have properly *qualified* your negotiating counterpart.

Qualifying a prospect is a well-known sales procedure.

For example, a salesman selling photocopying machines — prior to making any effort to sell the machine — will need to ensure that the prospective customer is in fact in the market (or at least has a need) for such a photocopying machine.

The process of qualifying is a legitimate and prudent business practice. For example, in a major tendering process, prospective tenderers will usually need to undergo a pre-qualification process to ensure that they meet certain minimum pre-requisites in relation to aspects of financial stability and service delivery capability.

As another example, if the party with which you are about to negotiate a sale of a business, has no finance, or if there are rumours in the marketplace that it has had trouble obtaining finance, then you may need to query whether the entire negotiation process will be worthwhile, or if there is a significant chance that it may be ultimately abortive.

One can sign a contract with virtually anybody. However, the more significant question is whether the other party is *likely* to be able to deliver what it has promised and whether that party will still be in existence in the years to come.

Qualification is a sensible risk management practice. It should be regarded as a normal part of the intelligence gathering process and background checking of your negotiating counterpart, in an attempt to learn as much as possible about them to determine their suitability and compatibility with your organisation's objectives.

For example, prior to entering into a contract with another company, it is good practice to conduct a search of the company with the appropriate companies registration authority (in most jurisdictions, this is a publicly searchable register).

Such a search may not only reveal whether the company exists under the name it has put forward to you, but may also reveal the presence of any charge (similar to a mortgage over a company) registered against the company or the existence of any writs, orders or bankruptcies affecting the company. This can often give an indication of other issues affecting (or even potentially crippling) the company and may give a better "feeling" in assessing the longer-term prospects of the company.

The search may also show if the company is under administration and that the officers of the company are powerless to enter into contracts of their own accord, without the administrator's consent.

Chapter 4

CULTURAL ASPECTS OF NEGOTIATION

■ ■ ■

Negotiating cultures

A basic understanding of the cultural issues surrounding negotiation is of fundamental importance. Indeed, without such knowledge, the only objectives you will be guaranteed of successfully achieving, are wasting everyone's time and embarrassing yourself.

Remember the old English proverb:

Zeal without knowledge is like fire without light.

This also applies to successful negotiation.

An understanding of these cultural differences will provide important clues to assist you in determining whether the persons with whom you are dealing, will have the requisite authority to do the deal, or, even that the company you are dealing with can approve of the deal on its own, without the requirement for its parent company approval.

A way of separating the differences in cultures is by examining the differing views to the following themes:

Cultures with hierarchical structures

Most Asian, European and middle-eastern cultures recognise and mark differences in status.

Unlike the English language, many other languages contain two forms of address for the word "you":

1)   one form is for formal use with strangers, superiors and subordinates; and

2)   the other form is reserved for more informal use with family, friends and for those colleagues that are seen as equals.

It is sometimes a difference that may not be appreciated by those in the English-speaking business world. For example, the janitor calling the CEO by their first name would not be something of note in Australia. Were this to occur in a European country, such as Italy or Spain, it would cause uproar.

In the hierarchical cultures, CEOs do not mix with the mailroom clerks. Any communication with a CEO from the lower ranks must follow the organisational chain of command. By the time any such message were to ever reach the CEO (if it ever did), it would have been subject to scrutiny, "filtering" and "censorship" through a number of hands on its way up the line. Any attempt to contact the CEO direct, by someone much further down the organisational chart, would be regarded as highly exceptional and perhaps even as an affront.

Cultures with egalitarian structures

Cultures in countries such as the United States of America or Australia tend to minimise the importance of status. Displays of status are also not openly encouraged or viewed favourably. As an example, many companies have done away with the reserved spaces for the CEO in the company car park.

Also, in many companies, the CEO holds "fireside chats" with lower management (or sometimes with the entire staff, depending upon the company's size) either by videoconference or email. Some organisations even internally publicise the CEO's email address, which any member of the company is invited to use to express his/her views or to offer comment or suggestion direct. The CEO would never be so "accessible" in a hierarchical culture.

In more egalitarian cultures, subordinates tend to view themselves as *equal* to their superiors. There is not the same deference shown to rank as there is in hierarchical cultures. One should therefore not be surprised to see the CEO of a company cooking a barbecue for the others at a company picnic.

Even in formal situations, people will tend to address one another by their first names, even upon a first meeting. As an example, even the most formal person may ask the chief executive of a multinational construction and excavation company, who is called Robert Katt, *Do you mind if I call you Bob?*

Cultures with a centralised mindset

Cultures with a centralised mindset are normally associated with hierarchical structures.

In these cultures, head office wants to know about and tightly regulate what is going on. Head office makes all of the important decisions. Delegation of authority is rare and if it happens, the limits of authority are quite low.

Independent actions and entrepreneurship are generally prohibited unless expressly permitted.

Cultures with a decentralised mindset

Cultures with a decentralised mindset are normally associated with egalitarian structures.

In these cultures, head office tends to delegate a lot of decision-making responsibility. Autonomy and entrepreneurship are encouraged and rewarded. Monitoring and controls imposed by head office are low (and in extreme cases, non-existent).

Independent actions and entrepreneurship are generally permitted unless expressly prohibited.

It is not unusual for the management in such situations to typically be left alone to their own devices, provided they are delivering the results expected. In this situation, the parent company tends to regard its subsidiary as an investment and will show more interest in the financial returns being generated, than with the business activities themselves — where it will regard the management as having the requisite expertise in that area. This mindset more often manifests itself where the subsidiary's business is *non-core* to the parent company's.

■■■

Cultural differences in practice

Since most cultures have different ways of conducting negotiations, it would be prudent to do some research to gain an appreciation of that culture, before entering into negotiations.

For example, when a Japanese person nods and says *yes* to you, you should not immediately think you have secured a firm and final agreement on that point. The person may simply be saying *yes* to acknowledge what you are saying and is not necessarily agreeing with your point.

A little basic knowledge of Japanese business etiquette will help avoid the highly damaging and embarrassing mistake of taking a Japanese person's business card single-handed, scribbling a note on it and then placing it in your back pocket and sitting down. It would be unwise to allow a person who saw nothing wrong with this picture, to travel to Japan and lead sensitive negotiations with a Japanese company.

It is prudent never make cultural assumptions about another person, based purely upon their appearance. For example, just because a person may appear to be Chinese, it might be unwise to draw that conclusion automatically. A second or third generation Australian (of Asian descent and appearance) might be highly offended at being consoled in the event of China's loss to Australia in a hotly contested Olympic swimming event. In fact, such a person described above may well consider themselves to be, firstly, Australian.

Some cultures are considerably more adept at negotiation. In fact, some cultures almost demand it in situations where negotiating and bargaining would appear inappropriate in other cultures.

For example, negotiators in some middle-eastern cultures, might approach you and ask you to quote a price on 20,000 units of a particular product. Naturally, such a large quantity would attract a significant discount over a much smaller order. If you do not first ascertain, in any depth, a genuine interest or capacity in placing such a large order and proceed to unwittingly give a price based on such a quantity, you might find that you are told:

Good we'll take 100 for now at a 15% reduction on the quoted price and talk later about more.

Hence, the outrageously high quantity is used as a negotiating ploy, to lure you into quoting a much lower price, than you otherwise would have. In such cultures, you may also find that time is a negotiating lever; protracting negotiations is used as a way to bring down your price.

Negotiation styles can also be culturally dependent as well. For example, a no-nonsense style of negotiating tends to be favoured in the USA. Such an approach might be viewed as overly aggressive in countries such as Japan, for example. The Japanese very much favour a relationship-based approach. Such a relationship tends to only be cultivated over time.

Obviously, some styles are incompatible and make negotiations much more difficult if the different approaches are not understood. For example, the methodical and committee-based Japanese approach may incorrectly be interpreted by Americans as a reluctance to do a deal.

Another example might be the differences between the initial warmth of Americans contrasted with the initial coldness or aloofness of some Asian or Middle-Eastern cultures. It has been said that Americans have a thin outer shell and a thick (and difficult to penetrate) inner core, whereas the other cultures mentioned tend to be the opposite. By breaking through the thick outer-shell of say an Asian, means you are then accepted into their "inner core".

Case study: Shall we settle this in court ... or over a drink?

There was an interesting study recently, underscoring the fundamental differences in the business cultures of the USA and Japan.

It compared the entertainment budgets and litigation budgets of a number of the largest companies in both countries. This was examined in the context of comparing commercial dispute resolution mechanisms.

The study concluded that in order to resolve commercial disputes the Japanese were much less litigation-prone than their US counterparts. Their litigation budgets were far *less* than those of their US counterparts, however, their entertainment budgets were far *higher*.

It has much to do with the Japanese concept of *maintaining face*. The Japanese were much more likely than their US counterparts, to settle their commercial disputes over dinner or during a lengthy session at a bar. Whereas Americans appeared to resort more to litigation, to resolve their disputes.

With certain Asian cultures, it is common for relatively junior persons within an organisation to be sent to have discussions with their negotiating counterpart. The danger for the counterpart is that such a tactic can effectively pave the way for two separate negotiations to be held.

Once a point is seemingly settled and agreed, the counterpart then learns of that the person who originally made the concession or concluded the agreement did not have the necessary authority to do so. Effectively, the previously "agreed" points are then thrown open for re-negotiation.

Cultural differences can have a significant impact even on contracts that have actually been entered into.

In relationship-dependent cultures, such as the Chinese culture, the contract is merely a signpost in the relationship. One should not therefore, be surprised at a request to renegotiate the terms of the contract. Making changes to a contract, *after it is signed*, is not an unusual thing for the Chinese, as they expect the dynamics of the relationship to prevail over any written document.

Of course, when we talk about culture, there is a grave risk of categorising people into compartments they may not fit into. The generalisations above can be used only as a starting point and a guide. Our knowledge of other cultures must then give way to the negotiating skills mentioned earlier, the ability to listen, communicate, empathise etc.

In the end, people are people — with all their attendant weaknesses, intricacies, idiosyncrasies and foibles.

■ ■ ■

Same language, different culture

Cultural diversity is not just about the differences between eastern and western cultures.

The British and American cultures can sometimes be a world apart. Hence, the old saying of the UK and the US being *two countries separated by a common language*. They have different accents, demeanours and expressions — even their systems of measurement are not the same.

One of the most conspicuous examples of such differences led to the loss of a $125 million Mars space probe in 1999. One group of engineers modelled navigation paths and trajectories using *pounds force* (the imperial measurement) while another group performed its calculations in *newtons* (the metric measurement). Incidentally, one *pound force* is the equivalent of approximately 4.45 *newtons*.

The result was that the changes made to the spacecraft's trajectory were actually 4.4 times greater than the navigation team had planned. The result caused the loss of the spacecraft.

Notwithstanding the common language of the engineers, misunderstandings still led to disaster.

Do not be tempted to think that cultural obstacles have to be significant in order to interfere with the accuracy and precision of your message.

Also relevant is the cultural problem of money.

An Australian referring to $1 billion dollars is substantially different to an American reference to the same amount; at the time of writing US$1 billion = A$1.68 billion. Furthermore, in Australia and England the word "billion" means "one million million". In the USA, the word "billion" means "one thousand million".

Such differences in understanding could prove disastrous in a commercial contract.

Thus, when it comes to drafting the contract, particular attention should be paid to the following matters:

- units of measurement to be adopted (metric or imperial);

- applicable currency;

- applicable language;

- jurisdiction;

- responsibility for currency and exchange rate fluctuations; and

- applicable time zone.

These issues are sometimes left for "someone else" to sort out as "mechanical" or minor issues.

It is a mistake to not pay careful attention to such matters.

For example, where a contract requires a crucial notice to be given by a particular time (especially in a situation where time is expressed to be of the essence), you do not want to be in a position where the notice should have been given by 4 pm Australian Eastern Standard time and you are giving the notice by 4 pm London time.

■ ■ ■

Doing business abroad — foreign corrupt practices laws

No discussion of the cultural aspects of negotiation is complete without a discussion of foreign corrupt practices legislation, enacted in a number of jurisdictions. Such legislation is used to combat the payment of bribes and secret commissions by companies to foreign officials in international business transactions.

The Problem

In some foreign countries, bribery in business is generally an accepted way of life, and may be regarded as a usual cost of doing business. A failure to pay a bribe could mean a failure to win business.

Foreign companies doing business in such countries may be faced with some form of corruption. However, it is not entirely fair to characterise all the officials and businesspeople of certain countries as being corrupt.

Many jurisdictions, until late last decade, allowed bribes paid overseas to be a tax-deductible expense. Such payments would not have been deductible expenses had they been paid in the company's home country. This legal double-standard had the effect of indirectly condoning such corruption abroad.

To deal more effectively with instances where companies doing business abroad encounter corruption, there is a need to have in place clear corporate policies giving guidance to management.

Consequences of the problem

A number of companies have tried to do business in these countries by taking the moral "high ground" and refusing to pay bribes. Many such companies reach the point where they are compelled to close down foreign branch offices and withdraw from doing business in the country.

Some countries have foreign-anti-corruption laws, while others refuse to introduce or enforce similar laws. In that instance, competitors based in such countries have a tangible advantage over their "corruption-legislated" counterparts. Indeed, one estimate, claimed that between 1994 and 1995, US companies lost over *$70 billion* in major overseas contracts — such losses being *solely* attributable to the corrupt practices of the other contract bidders.

Foreign anti-corruption laws

The USA was the one of the first countries to pass anti-corruption laws of this nature. In 1977 it introduced the *Foreign Corrupt Practices Act*, which has since been codified into the *Securities Exchange Act*.

In 1999, Australia also enacted, what some might argue, was a somewhat diluted form of such legislation: the *Criminal Code Amendment (Bribery of Foreign Public Officials) Act* 1999 (Cth). In that same year, Australia also amended its tax laws to end the practice of claiming tax deductions for such payments made abroad.

Some jurisdictions (such as Australia) also have a form of Secret Commissions Act designed to prohibit a person from offering secret commissions to an agent or an employee. Such legislation can even go so far as prohibiting an agent from accepting a gift or inducement likely to influence the agent to do an act on behalf of a principal.

Such laws, generally, make it an offence to provide, promise or cause the offer of a benefit to another person, with the intention of:

- influencing a foreign public official to obtain or retain business; and/or

- obtaining or retaining an improper advantage.

The definition "foreign public official" may include foreign government employees and contractors. It can sometimes even extend to employees of foreign public enterprises.

Penalties

Penalties vary from jurisdiction to jurisdiction. They can include fines for individuals and for corporations and/or provide for terms of imprisonment, or both.

Ancillary offences

Ancillary offences may include attempting, aiding, abetting, procuring, urging or conspiring to commit an offence.

A director or senior executive may commit an ancillary offence if he or she causes a benefit to be provided, or, is aware of the circumstances of the payment and does not intervene to prevent it.

Limits on the scope of such laws

In some jurisdictions, there may be exemptions or defences available for payments sanctioned by the law in the foreign public official's country, for "minor" facilitation benefits made in respect of "routine government actions".

Whereas, other jurisdictions go further and may define bribes to include such "consultant fees" and other similar "facilitation payments" — regardless of the label actually applied to such payments.

Naturally, it is important that you obtain up to date and qualified advice concerning such matters *both* in the particular jurisdiction in which you are based and the one in which you are considering doing business.

Chapter 5

PREPARING TO NEGOTIATE — APPROACH AND STRATEGY

■ ■ ■

Positional v collaborative bargaining

Commercial contract negotiation demands the application of a combination of negotiating skill and legal flair.

The use of a positional approach involves the negotiator asking three questions in preparation for the negotiation:

1) ***What is my bottom line?*** This will largely determine at what point to open.

2) ***Where do I open?*** This will depend on the bottom line point.

3) ***What series of "give and take" steps are needed to move from opening to conclusion so as to end as far above the bottom line as possible?*** This will depend on the time available and the size of the gap between the opening and bottom line positions.

Bottom line

The "bottom line", in this context, is the point at which it is no longer economically viable to continue the negotiation.

Opening point

The opening point can influence the approach to be adopted by the other side and may even be a determining factor in whether a negotiation will conclude with a successful result. Much will depend on the personalities of your counterparts.

Case study: pulling the rug from under you

You spot a particularly attractive Turkish rug at a bazaar in Istanbul. You realise that this would suit your living room better than anything you have ever seen.

You decide that you *really* want the rug.

The seller asks for $100 and you respond with a lowball counter-offer of $5.

The seller might then say he will give you a great price, as you are his friend (notwithstanding the fact that you have only just met), will let you have it "for a mere $50".

You maintain a friendly rapport the whole time and neither of you is insulted by the outrageously high opening offer or outrageously low counter-offer.

You decide to pursue this over a cup of tea. During the next 20 minutes you move up incrementally, while he comes down by similar increments.

Eventually, you come to a mutually agreeable $20 and secure the rug of your dreams.

With some, a "lowball" opening offer (an unrealistically low one) may be expected by the other side and is usually met with an unrealistically high demand from the other side. This "tennis match" approach (to and fro) is usually long-winded, but given enough time and good-will between the parties, can ultimately deliver a result.

However, with a different personality type on the other side, an unrealistically low opening position can unnecessarily antagonise the other side and cause them to form the view that you are not really serious about negotiating.

In such a case, the Turkish rug scenario could have turned out entirely differently — with the store owner cursing you and chasing you out of his store at the mere suggestion that one of his prized rugs could be worth a paltry $5.

"Laying all the cards on the table"

Depending upon the situation and the personalities involved, some negotiators will open with a *laying all the cards on the table* approach. That is, by holding nothing back and making the first and final offer, giving cogent reasons explaining the position.

Again, much of this approach is personality-dependent.

It is more likely to work where two experienced negotiators, who know and trust each other well, meet.

Otherwise, the real risk is that there are those who will view your position with scepticism — still thinking that you have "a little more in reserve". The *laying all the cards on the table* approach will rarely work with such personality types, who will always require the concession to feel they have achieved a "win".

To open with this approach and to *then* make further concessions could be fatal to your credibility. See more about this aspect in the section on **Credibility**.

Allowing for some hold back

The more conventional opening approach is to allow for some limited hold back.

This gives you the opportunity to survey the mood of the negotiations and to get a better feel for the personality of your negotiating counterpart.

It is much easier to ease and concede a little from your present position than it is to try and resile from it.

Exploring the "why" behind the other party's position

The following case study of a negotiation over an important contract clause — with significant ramifications for both parties — is a useful demonstration of how a collaborative effort can achieve a benefit to both parties in a contract.

Case study: how collaborative negotiation solved the Year 2000 problem

While the issue of the Year 2000 (Y2K) problem has long gone, it provided many useful opportunities for contract negotiation objectives to be brought to the fore.

At the time, it was a very real issue for businesses — primarily because no one actually knew what was going to happen. That uncertainty brought with it fear and (on occasion) overcompensation in planning for the event.

A point of contention for many service providers was whether Y2K circumstances would constitute an event that relieved a service provider from its obligations under a contract (without penalty) for the duration of the event (a *force majeure* event).

For example, for contract cleaning firms engaged to clean office buildings, it was an interesting (and recurring) dilemma.

The cleaning company was generally able to assure its customer that if the worst-case scenario of doom occurred, the core services of "mops and buckets" would not be affected. However, if the cleaning company's computers irretrievably crashed, then incidental matters such as invoicing, the cleaning company's payroll etc would be adversely affected.

Given the customer's primary preoccupation was having its buildings cleaned, then Y2K would not be a problem. As long as the customer was willing to tolerate manual (or even handwritten invoicing), then the services would not be adversely compromised.

The only qualification to the assurance that "the mops and buckets would always be there" was the possibility that Y2K might:

- cause traffic gridlock and stop the cleaners actually getting to the sites; or

- cause the building's doors to lock, preventing access to buildings.

> Customers invariably understood the concerns as such scenarios were often a realistic part of the customer's own Y2K problem planning.
>
> With those objectives in mind, parties were able to conclude deals that accommodated the needs and concerns of both parties.

In the above example, positional negotiation would not have achieved anything. What brought about a solution in that situation was the fact that the parties were willing to explore the real needs behind the objectives of each party.

Otherwise, in a strictly positional approach, one party would have simply demanded that Y2K be made a *force majeure* event and the other party would have strongly resisted. A deal could have stalled or possibly even have been lost if the parties had simply adopted and maintained their positions firmly, without making an effort to understand the why behind the other party's position. To read more about the operation of *force majeure* clauses see **Understanding Commonly Used Contract Terms: Boilerplate Clauses**, the fourth volume in the *Commercial Contracts for Managers Series*.

Where all objectives were clearly expressed, it was possible to accommodate the needs of each party, without necessarily compromising those of the other.

Case study:
a father and loud music

A guide to peaceful coexistence

Consider a simple example of a situation involving a young girl **Kiara** and her father, **Frank**.

Frank wants to have a peaceful and quiet environment in his house, in order to concentrate on writing more best-selling books about commercial contracts.

On the other hand, **Kiara** wants to have an afternoon of listening to her favourite music, with the volume turned up to a considerably high level, in order to "truly experience" the music.

Both **Frank** and **Kiara's** individual requirements appear, on their face, to be completely and totally contradictory and incompatible. **Frank** has no desire to "truly experience" such music.

One of them cannot achieve what they want without upsetting and causing the other to "lose".

> If **Frank** had taken a hardline, asserted his authority over the situation and ordered her not to play any music, **Kiara** would have seen **Frank** to be a "bully". Such an approach would also not have stood **Frank** in good stead and maintained their relationship, especially for future similar negotiations.
>
> If the parties had focused on their *positions* rather than a mutually satisfactory outcome, **Frank** might never have thought to hand **Kiara** a pair of headphones.
>
> Instead, by **Frank** thinking of *how he could accommodate her wants — without necessarily compromising on his position* — a solution was found that gave them both a "win", by each of them getting what it was they originally wanted.

It is far easier (and demands little or no skill) to walk into a negotiation, state your demands and say "no" to anything that does not satisfy those demands; or alternatively, to "beat" the other side into submission. Such actions are not usually "tough" but merely demonstrate inflexibility and lack of imagination.

It is far harder (and requires far more skill, inventiveness and imagination) to reach an outcome satisfactory to two competing interests. There are also considerable dividends obtained from building relationships and generating good-will that will be of benefit in future negotiations.

Collaborative bargaining tends to accentuate the common ground existing between the parties and to look for the shared interest. The focus is centred upon *interests*, rather than respective *positions*.

Recitals

When it comes to drafting the contract, these interests can sometimes be set out in the contract, as *recitals*.

Recitals set the background and help give some context to the transaction the subject of the contract. They can be a convenient way of recording the parties' intentions, which could become valuable interpretation tools for a court in the event of a dispute.

■■■

Relationships in a negotiation

The building of relationships is important in any constructive negotiation process. Indeed, many parties invest much time and effort to help achieve that end.

However, one must not lose sight of the fact that negotiating still remains — to a certain extent — a somewhat adversarial process, involving "us" and "them". There are times where you will reach a point in negotiations where one party can only gain something, at the other party's expense (win–lose).

It is wise to also remember that the people negotiating the deal are generally not the same as those who will actually execute the operational terms of the contract. Contracts often endure beyond the corporate lifespan of the persons who originally negotiated the deal — as people either leave or are promoted within a company.

For these reasons, some safeguards are necessary to protect you from "getting too close" in the ultimate contractual relationship, resulting from the concluded bargain of the parties. A prime example would be a situation where the parties agree to work in *partnership* to solve a particular problem or produce a desired outcome. To express this as a *partnership,* might be true in a conversational or colloquial sense, however, the parties might not intend to actually become "partners" in the *legal* sense of the word.

Another example might be, an instance where the parties expect one another to act in *good faith* in their dealings with the other. In such a situation, it would be imprudent to assume that the law will impose such an obligation, in all jurisdictions.

Note that, most of the time, these fundamental relationship issues may not explicitly arise *during* the negotiation. Such issues usually tend to appear "on paper", for the first time, in a draft of the contract document. As such, these issues may be relegated to "second-rate" status, in the minds of the parties. A time-conscious executive might be tempted to think:

If these issues were important, we would have covered them during the negotiation.

It can be a dangerous practice to allow yourself to be lured into such a trap. The reason such issues are not commonly raised or discussed during a negotiation is that their effect hinges very much on the way they are drafted into a contract.

This is one of the reasons why it is wise to seek to have control of the meeting agenda and/or the contract drafting process, wherever possible. See more about this issue in the section **Who draws the contracts?** in Chapter 10.

It is important that these relationship aspects be kept at the back of your mind during the negotiation process.

This will cause you to be alert to any subtle reference to them, or some other cue, during the negotiation discussions. Otherwise, when you object to the point appearing in the contract, you risk the other party affirming that the matter was indeed "touched upon" during the negotiations and that you offered no opposition to the point — therefore, that they were justifiably entitled to assume that you had agreed (or at least did not have any opposition) to the point.

These relationship factors all contribute to influencing the risk and potential liability profile of the deal. We will proceed to examine three of the more important and commonly arising ones.

With the exception of the first of them, the issues selected for closer examination have a common theme: they all strongly influence the apportionment of (or sometimes, the complete exoneration of a party from) liability.

All of the issues are sufficiently powerful, in their own right, to "turn around" an otherwise "good" contract into one that is unprofitable, unworkable or even a financial disaster.

Obligation to act reasonably

In the USA, it is common for contracts to expressly impose an obligation of good faith and fair dealing upon the parties to that contract.

If this is a requirement for you to make the contract workable, it is important that you consider this at the negotiation stage to ensure that no one has any fundamental objections to such a clause appearing in the final contract document. Whilst the drafting might still be debated, securing an agreement to the concept is a major step forward.

In most jurisdictions, in the absence of a special relationship — such as that of employer/employee or insurer/insured — there appears to be no general or uniform obligation in contract law for arm's-length commercial parties to a contract, to act reasonably. Under certain circumstances in some jurisdictions, however, this duty may be implied. Note also, that depending upon the jurisdiction, a court may be entitled to imply such a term, even if the contract expressly excludes all implied terms.

The question remains, what does it mean to act "reasonably"? A typical lawyer's answer would be that it depends on the circumstances. It might be suggested that acting "reasonably" is to act within the "spirit" of the agreement. However, a cynic might suggest it is "whatever you can get away with", without breaching a contract or being accused of being fraudulent.

Assume there are two parties to a contract: the Contractor providing a particular service or services to the Principal. In many contracts, especially government contracts, the Contracts Administrator (appointed by and representing the Principal) has very wide and extensive powers. On occasion, the personality of the Contract Administrator can have a substantial effect on the working relationship with the Contractor. In extreme cases, the effects of the Contract Administrator's actions could even have a potentially detrimental impact on the Contractor's profitability.

To overcome the potential effects, upon a Contractor, of the actions of a hostile Contracts Administrator, the inclusion — into a contract — of the a clause similar to the following, can be a useful negotiating tool:

> *Wherever the Principal or Contract Administrator is required to make any decision or determination, give any direction, exercise any discretion, form any opinion, give any interpretation or exercise any powers, it shall at all times act reasonably and do so upon reasonable grounds.*

Remember that without such a clause, once the contract is signed, no amount of pleading "please be reasonable!" can then assist you.

This area of the law is still developing in some jurisdictions, such as New South Wales.

You would do well to assume that a court in your jurisdiction would not be prepared to imply any obligation to act reasonably, in relation to a Principal's exercise of any powers conferred by the contract.

In jurisdictions where the duty is not implied, a court might not consider that such a duty is necessary for the proper commercial operation of the contract.

Golden Rule

If you expect or require the other party to the contract to have to act reasonably in its dealings with you, you should raise this at the negotiation stage and ask for it to be *explicitly* stated in the contract.

Partnership at law and in "sales-speak"

As always, in the sales documents, meetings, negotiations and presentations, one is operating in "sales mode" in an attempt to win favour with, and impress, a customer or prospective customer.

On the other hand, the customer is trying to maximise its benefits in a deal, hoping that competing sales people "pull out all stops" to outdo one another.

You may, at one time or another, encounter an unscrupulous salesperson who regards it as their job to find, persuade, convince and to sell — in any way they can: *Whatever it takes to get across the line*, is their motto. *Legal matters will take care of themselves*, is their hope. Such a salesperson is the one with which you will need to exercise the most care and caution.

When in sales mode, a party will do all that it can to make the customer feel good and secure about its purchasing decision. One method currently in vogue is the idea that the organisation selling a product or service will work together in a *partnership* to achieve the customer's goals.

This expression may be acceptable to use in conversational terms. However, at law, partnerships carry with them an altogether different significance.

At law, a partnership carries some onerous obligations.

- **The ability to bind other partners jointly and severally.**

  The most significant is the ability of *one* partner to make a commitment or enter into an undertaking that *jointly and severally* binds the other partners (even without the knowledge of the other partners).

- **The *fiduciary* nature of the relationship.**

  A relationship is said to be a *fiduciary relationship* where someone is in a position of trust in relation to another (or others) and who must, therefore, act for that person's (or those persons') benefit.

  A *fiduciary* must avoid any situation where that fiduciary could have a personal interest conflicting (or which might conflict) with the interests of those whom the *fiduciary* is bound to protect.

  A *fiduciary relationship* generally exists between a solicitor and his/her client, a director and the company on whose board that director sits and between partners in a partnership.

Clearly, such onerous obligations are not usually the intention of two parties on "opposing" sides contracting at arm's-length.

Non-binding statement of partnership

One should also exercise caution with some forms of the *non-binding statement of partnership*.

This has become an increasingly common feature of some service contracts, in tendering situations. For example, some of these consist of flowery statements of how the parties will continue to co-operate and "love" one another. Then comes "the crunch" — when the statement is expressed to be binding *only* upon the seller, but *non-binding* upon the customer.

Therefore, when a seller attempts to exercise or enforce any rights against the customer, the "shield" of "partnership" is raised against the seller. A seller attempting to assert rights against a customer by the use of litigation will, no doubt, be met by a customer's claims that an approach using any kind of "force" is inconsistent with the notion that the parties are partners working co-operatively together.

However, if the customer has occasion to exercise any right against the seller, it can cheerfully proceed to do so with impunity and without remorse. Such a "partnership" obligation applies only unilaterally upon the seller.

The enforceability and real effect of such a "partnership" statement may be questionable in some jurisdictions.

Golden Rule

Beware of the "non-binding statement of partnership".

If confronted by one, be sure to carefully read and fully understand the implications of any such statement before accepting and signing it.

Joint and several liability

This is relevant where there are two or more parties on one side of a deal. That is, where there are two or more persons (or companies) as one party to a contract.

For example, where there are two or more entities providing a service to a customer, or where two or more parties are borrowing money from a lender.

For reasons, which will soon become apparent, joint and several liability is something which *must* be dealt with at the negotiation stage. This is not just a drafting point "for the lawyers to sort out".

For such a clause to simply appear in a draft of a contract for services (without any prior discussion), is something likely to cause a fundamental difference between the parties.

Whereas, the appearance of a joint and several liability clause in a draft of a contract for the lease of a property or in a mortgage contract, would likely not even attract attention, as these clauses are customary inclusions in such types of transactions. Indeed, in such cases, their *omission* would probably cause more surprise.

For the purposes of the following example, let us make the following assumptions:

1) The parties to a contract are: **Mega Co** and **Tiny Co** (as the first party) both providing services to **Suham** (the second party).

2) The contract provides that: "**Mega Co** and **Tiny Co** shall be *jointly and severally* liable to **Suham**".

3) **Tiny Co** breaches the contract and causes **Suham** loss.

4) **Mega Co** has not breached the contract.

In practice, **Mega Co** and **Tiny Co** being both jointly and severally liable to **Suham**, effectively means:

- **Suham** would be entitled to sue *either or both Mega Co* or **Tiny Co** for the recovery of the *full amount* of **Suham's** loss.

- **Suham** would *not* be restricted to suing only **Tiny Co** to recover its loss. *Without* a joint and several liability clause, it would be so restricted.

- **Suham** does *not* need to sue each of **Mega Co** and **Tiny Co** to recover half of its loss from each of them — in separate actions.

It is significant to understand the concept of joint and several liability, as it enables **Suham** to choose to sue only **Mega Co** to recover all of its loss — even if **Tiny Co** went into liquidation or receivership. In that case, it would then be up to **Mega Co** to try and sue **Tiny Co** to attempt to recover its share of loss.

When used thoughtfully, such a simple phrase can have very powerful effects. When being used against you, you should exercise great caution.

If used against you (and one or more other parties to a contract), you need to carefully consider:

1) How similar are the interests of these parties to become jointly and severally liable? For example, does one hold a 1% stake in the outcome and in return face a potential 100% risk?

2) The respective means of each of the parties to become jointly and severally liable. By this, we intend the *actual* means, rather than the *apparent* ones. For example, there are many subsidiary companies of large household-name groups of companies that may be technically insolvent. The only way they maintain solvency is with parent company support. If that support stops, the subsidiary "dies" (along with your prospects of seeking any contribution for their share).

3) The stability of the other parties. Take heed of the favourite statement used in the securities and investment industry: *past performance is no indicator or guarantee of future returns.*

It might be appropriate to mention at this point, a misconception amongst a small number of managers; that a mere reference to an entity within the body of a document is sufficient to bind that entity to an enforceable obligation — even if that entity is not actually a party to the contract. This is, quite clearly, *not* the case.

Golden Rule

You should only agree to accept joint and several liability with another party (or parties), if you are prepared to assume 100% of the liability.

■ ■ ■

Building trust

Building trust in negotiations is a vital process. The absence of such trust often leads to a waste of precious time and energy as points and statements made need to be tested and verified before they are accepted.

Trust can be built in a number of ways. One way might be by initially providing information that can be proven and perhaps by making small concessions as a sign of good faith in achieving the deal co-operatively.

When a party gives away something to another, it creates a feeling of obligation upon that other party to reciprocate — from there they too start to give. After an exchange, a degree of trust begins to build.

Credibility is an important factor necessary to establishing trust — this was discussed in greater detail in Chapter 2. Also, demonstrating a genuine interest in achieving a win–win solution (by your actions rather than just words), is another way to establishing trust.

However, as with loyalty, there is no fast-track to building trust. It must be earned ... over time. Realise also that once established, it becomes a valuable asset and should not be treated lightly or taken for granted; trust built over many years can be destroyed (or at least seriously damaged) in a single instant by an error in judgment. This can be more of a problem for a large organisation, whose hard-won reputation over many years can lay in the hands of those few individuals representing it. Any misdeed by one of those persons, can have severe repercussions throughout the organisations and can unfairly taint all those persons within it.

This is another reason to select with great care, those persons who will be representing your organisation to the rest of the world.

Establishing rapport in a negotiation is an important step in developing the trust necessary to forge negotiating relationships. However, there are limits.

Beware the negotiator who tries too hard to be your best friend. In such a situation, it can pay to ask yourself *Why?*

It is an established influencing technique that you are much more likely to gain acceptance of a proposition you are advancing, if the person you are trying to convince regards you as trustworthy or as a friend. The aim is to have the people you are trying to convince, internally overcome their own inherent scepticism by thinking to themselves: *Why would that person lie to me? They are my friend.*

An indicator of this type of behaviour can sometimes occur during the negotiation when you are asked by a smiling enquirer:

Where are you from?

OR

How many children do you have?

Naturally, you should avoid going to the other extreme of attributing a sinister motive to someone who is merely making an attempt to be cordial and civil towards you.

■ ■ ■

Planning for the negotiation

It is true that preparation gives confidence, but it can also give the edge in a negotiation.

Many of you may be familiar with the scene in the movie *Wall Street* (1987), where Michael Douglas' character, Gordon Gekko, quotes the words of ancient Chinese philosopher, Sun Tzu to his young protégé:

Most battles are won and lost before they are ever fought.

This can be true of negotiations.

Conversely, an old military adage says that:

War plans never survive their first contact with reality.

This can also indeed be true of negotiations.

It is, therefore, important to take both of these concepts into consideration when formulating your negotiating objectives and preparing your negotiating plan.

You must take the time to prepare such plans and objectives, but keep them sufficiently flexible so they can evolve — as contingencies arise or events take an unexpected turn — during the negotiation.

Checklist: negotiation preparation

There are a number of matters vital to preparing for a final negotiation.

At a minimum, one would be required to have an in-depth familiarity and knowledge of the:

- ☑ relevant facts, figures and issues concerning the subject matter of the negotiation;

- ☑ outcome you seek and whether it is realistically achievable;

- ☑ respective strengths and weaknesses of both your own and the other side's situation and how this influences the parties' respective bargaining strengths — have you played "devil's advocate" in relation to your own stance on particular issues of significance?;

- ☑ key drivers influencing the other side;

- ☑ personalities representing the other side;

- ☑ level of authority for each side (will the persons present be the actual decision-makers?);

- ☑ right team members available for all parties at the negotiation, where commercial/technical decisions will need to made or discussed (eg, tax issues, engineering issues etc);

- ☑ agenda for the meeting;

- ☑ strategy and tactics to be adopted;

- ☑ opening stance or position;

- ☑ any particular or unusual advantage or disadvantage affecting either party (eg, a particular time constraint);

- ☑ alternative plan of action, if the negotiation is not successful or reaches a point at which you must walk away; and

- ☑ ranking of the relevant issues to establish their importance in light of achieving the final objective (we'll proceed to cover this point next).

The negotiating team needs to consider how the agenda should look *before* the first meeting. Wherever possible, control over the preparation of any agenda should be sought. This can sometimes be one of the advantages of home turf.

Many, of course, tend to focus on a forthcoming negotiation from their own (sometimes narrow) perspective. They might clearly see their own strengths but can sometimes tend to dedicate an inordinate amount of time focusing *only* upon their weaknesses. Let's not misunderstand the point: spending *some* time planning for and around weaknesses in your own position, is prudent and a sensible practice.

It is a good practice to also closely examine the *other* party's situation; their strengths and weaknesses.

It can sometimes be of assistance to a team if there is some role play with one of the negotiation team acting the part of the other party. This can be a useful way of preventing a party from unnecessary pessimism: *Our position is weak — we have to make concessions.*

■ ■ ■

Proper ranking of issues

Rarely will it be necessary to fight every issue "to the death" in a negotiation. A party does not need to be a negotiating "bully" and win *every* negotiated point, in order to arrive at a bargain with which they can live.

Some points are deliberately raised by a party only as negotiation points — which can later be safely conceded, in exchange for similar concessions from the other side. It is good practice to have some of these points available, without exaggerating the process, of course.

A point to note about concessions: when one is given, most will require another one to be given in return. When "trading" concessions, however, it is important they be of roughly equivalent value: a major concession from one side should be exchanged with one of a similar magnitude, from the other side. Otherwise, one risks "giving away the farm" in return for a string of inconsequential concessions cheerfully volunteered by the other side.

In advance of the negotiation, it is necessary (as well as extremely helpful) to map out all of the issues and discuss them thoroughly both internally and with the relevant advisors.

Decisions need to be made on whether to tackle the easier issues first (to obtain some immediate consensus and build trust) or whether it is more appropriate to discuss the hard issues first — to ascertain whether a deal will even be possible, before delving into the detail.

It is a useful pre-negotiation exercise to reach internal agreement on the categorisation of these issues. In practice, there are three effective categories of deal points.

TABLE 1: RANKING NEGOTIATION ISSUES

Points to easily concede	Points that may be conceded if necessary	Points that cannot be conceded under any circumstances

It actually helps to put them down on paper, using the above format, during internal discussions to establish the organisation's position on each item.

It is important that the number of points in the third column be kept to an absolute minimum. These points are the *deal-breakers*, ie, points over which you are willing to end the negotiations and "walk away".

The process of preparing the list really focuses the persons involved on the important issues.

Therefore, the team knows, in advance, which issues merit the greater investment of time and effort and which issues do not.

Preparing the list can be a particularly gruelling process in a major transaction, but can pay dividends during the negotiation.

Naturally, the completed version of the above list is highly confidential. The persons with knowledge of the contents of the list should be restricted to those with an absolute need-to-know. For obvious reasons, it is vital that hard or electronic copies not be liberally circulated or made available. See also the section on **Security of your information**.

■ ■ ■

Negotiating strategy

The strategy chosen must be a suitable fit to the circumstances. The strategy that was of benefit to you in last week's negotiation, will not necessarily be so this week.

Strategy is a combination of the negotiating style to be used (confrontational or co-operative) and the approach you intend to adopt (whether positional or collaborative). We'll examine the differences in approaches in the next section.

Adopting a single strategy for a negotiation is often the hallmark of inexperience, as it risks making you too inflexible.

An ideal strategy needs to be able to *evolve* in response to changes during the negotiation. Remember that the balance of bargaining power can often shift during the negotiation.

Your strategy needs to conform to this level of fluidity in events.

Golden Rule

Remember that longer-term contracts often require a different negotiating perspective to those of a shorter-term nature, that do not depend upon a relationship being established and developed.

■ ■ ■

Security of your information

An often-neglected aspect of negotiation is the maintenance of adequate security measures to safeguard valuable commercial information. A competitor having access to such information can have a valuable and significant advantage over you.

Imagine how much easier your task would be if you knew your negotiating counterpart's "bottom line"!

Basic sensible and practical measures can be undertaken to implement fundamental protection.

Physical security of information

One must be prepared to judge the circumstances of each particular situation in order to draw a line between prudence and paranoia.

Obviously security issues tend to become more problematic when you are away from your home territory. Especially, if you are in an unfamiliar country, where the language and cultural differences may place you at a disadvantage. For example, in some countries there is a trade in sensitive commercial information obtained through hotel staff copying faxes or cleaning staff examining the contents of your briefcase.

One can take precautions as basic and simple as locking briefcases in hotel rooms or not leaving papers or files in a negotiation room as the parties go to lunch.

Also, open discussions in public places represent one of the greatest security threats. On trains, buses, aeroplanes (one of the most frequently occurring lapses) or even hotel foyers people tend to be more relaxed about such matters; they think that "no one will be listening" or if they are "they won't understand" their language.

In particular high-risk situations (especially in certain countries), one must step-up security measures to extend beyond normal thinking — to assume that rooms and/or telephones might be bugged. One should maintain the highest levels of discretion and strictly limit (or preferably avoid) communication with head office on the progress of the negotiations.

In fact, companies regularly engaged in negotiations in high risk environments, should have in place clear policies and procedures dealing with these issues.

Even for non-high risk companies, it is basic common sense to ensure that your executives do not engage in discussions about sensitive issues in places where they are likely to be overheard — such as on board an aeroplane. Such a statement may appear to be blindingly obvious, but how many times have you been able to overhear such a discussion? On board a flight, there may be a varied and captive audience all around you. One just never knows when one of them could be a staff member of a competitor or an advisor to a competitor, eagerly taking note of your every word.

These topics are rarely given a second thought in our own insular and cosy environments, where such tactics tend to be the stuff one only reads about in spy thrillers. That is, until a major security breach occurs. In which case, a company is then faced with counting the cost of such a lapse and usually spares no expense in implementing more stringent security measures and policies for the future.

■■■

Maintaining confidentiality

Parties who do not know one another or who have never previously dealt with one another, need to be certain — to the fullest extent possible — that certain commercially sensitive information to be passed to another, either in anticipation of or during a negotiation, will only be used for a limited and specified purpose.

Such agreements are usually put in place prior to the commencement of a negotiation. This enables the flow of information to commence — the intention being that the information provided will then be the subject of a negotiated deal.

A confidentiality agreement is usually the best method to prevent the improper use of information by the party receiving it, who attempts to gain or exploit an unfair advantage, through the use of such information.

Confidentiality agreements can themselves be the subject of intense negotiations over their terms. The following is a checklist of the drafting points to cover in a basic confidentiality agreement.

Checklist: elements of a basic confidentiality agreement
Questions to consider and specify in a confidentiality agreement
• What is to be considered "confidential information"?   • For what specific purpose will the information be supplied?   • Are there to be any exceptions to the definition of "confidential information"?   • Are there to be any permissible disclosures?
Positive statements to be made
That: • disclosure is not intended to transfer any rights in such information;   • there is no exclusivity to the Recipient in the confidential information;   • there is no obligation upon the Discloser to provide confidential information;   • the supply of confidential information does not constitute an offer; and   • no warranty is given about the accuracy or completeness of the information.

Checklist: elements of a basic confidentiality agreement —

continued

Statements of the recipient's obligations
The Recipient of the confidential information: • shall use all reasonable measures to keep the information confidential; • shall be responsible for any unauthorised disclosure; • indemnifies the Discloser for loss arising from the Recipient's breach of the agreement (this is an optional requirement); • acknowledges that breach of the agreement may cause loss to the Discloser; • shall return all confidential information on demand; and • agrees not to solicit or approach employees, customers or suppliers.
Other terms
• Term of the agreement. How long is the agreement to be in force? When does it start? When does it end? • Governing law and jurisdiction. Under what state or country's law will the agreement be enforced?

Increasingly, disclosing parties are tending to push for the inclusion of the following additional terms in confidentiality agreements.

An exclusivity provision

An *exclusivity provision* is designed to "lock-in" a period during which the Discloser of confidential information cannot enter into a contract with any other party during the exclusivity period. To broaden the concept further, it might be appropriate for the clause to provide that the Discloser shall not provide any information to or hold any discussions with any other party during the exclusivity period.

The typical reason for requesting an exclusivity provision is where the Recipient of confidential information is about to embark on an expensive investigation exercise (such as a *due diligence* on the acquisition of a business) prior to making a firm commitment (executing a contract) to proceed with a transaction.

Because of the time required and the expense needed to be outlaid for the process, the Recipient will want to be certain that those monies expended will not be wasted because the "rug was pulled from under them", by the Discloser selling the business to another party before the Recipient had concluded its investigations and had the opportunity to make a final decision.

Case study: here are your handcuffs ...

The CEO of **Cobra Enterprises** is in discussions with the CEO of **Tusk Limited**.

- **Cobra** wishes to enter into a transaction with **Tusk** for the purchase of **Tusk's** telecommunications subsidiary, **Trunk Systems**.

- As part of the evaluation process, **Cobra** proposes to embark upon a full due diligence of **Trunk Systems**.

- **Cobra** estimates the due diligence process will take approximately six weeks and cost in the order of $500,000.

- To safeguard its position, **Cobra** requires a period of exclusivity on the deal for eight weeks, until it has been able to complete the due diligence and conduct other necessary assessments and evaluations.

- **Cobra** does not want to devote time and money to a process where **Tusk** could be holding discussions with another party/ies for the same deal. **Cobra** also wants to be sure there are no other competitors making a bid, which would help drive up the price of the business.

- **Tusk** agrees to grant **Cobra** an *exclusivity period*, effectively tying-up **Tusk**.

- The draft of the *exclusivity agreement* provides that **Tusk** will not to sign an agreement for the sale of **Trunk Systems** with any other party before the expiry of the eight-week exclusivity period.

- However, **Cobra** goes one step further in asking that **Tusk** also agree *not to hold discussions with or enter negotiations* with any other party during the exclusivity period.

This additional restriction, preventing **Tusk** from holding discussions with anyone else, could considerably weaken **Tusk's** bargaining position with **Cobra**.

By retaining the ability to negotiate with other prospective purchasers, **Tusk** places pressure upon **Cobra** to complete the purchase of **Trunk Systems** within the time-limit of the exclusivity period. If it fails to do so, **Cobra** risks the possibility that **Tusk** could sign a deal with another purchaser, on the day following the expiry of the exclusivity period. Such pressure reduces any negotiating leverage that **Cobra** might have otherwise had against **Tusk**. It also minimises the effect upon **Tusk** of any minor issues uncovered by **Cobra** during due diligence.

Whereas, if **Cobra** was certain that **Tusk** had not engaged in negotiations with anyone else during the exclusivity period, **Cobra** would gain the upper hand.

Cobra could more easily "drag-out" the negotiations beyond the exclusivity period with impunity — knowing full well that **Tusk** had yet to even commence the negotiation process with any other party.

> This would tend to give **Cobra** additional bargaining power in negotiations with **Tusk** — knowing that **Tusk** would need to start the entire sale process from the beginning.
>
> The situation would be much worse for **Tusk**, where **Tusk** was under some kind of time-related pressure to conclude a deal.

When asked by the Recipient to include an exclusivity provision in an agreement, it may be appropriate, in some circumstances, to require that a *break-fee* provision be included. A *break-fee*, typically, is a non-refundable payment to be made to the Discloser by the Recipient of confidential information, in the event that the Recipient does not proceed with the transaction, after the expiration of the exclusivity period.

The *break-fee* concept may help determine whether a Recipient is serious in its intentions and that its request for exclusivity is a genuine one, or whether the exclusivity request is merely indiscriminate and purely designed to create a tactical delay for the Discloser; for example, by keeping a business the Discloser is trying to sell "off the market", for the duration of the exclusivity period.

A non-solicitation provision

A non-solicitation provision is sometimes called an anti-poaching provision and is often one of the most sensitive and valuable issues to a Discloser. A Discloser does not want a Recipient to capitalise (to the detriment of the Discloser) upon knowledge of customer or supplier lists and details of key employees. This is particularly so where the Recipient may be a direct competitor of the Discloser.

Often exceptions are included in such clauses where the solicitation occurs purely coincidentally (in a large company for example) and that such persons engaged in the solicitation of an employee, have no knowledge of the confidential information.

Exceptions are also common dealing with instances where an employee voluntarily responds to a publicly placed job advertisement.

For a more comprehensive treatment of confidentiality agreements and examples of their use, you should consult *Understanding Confidentiality Agreements*, the second volume in the *Commercial Contract for Managers Series*.

Chapter 6

DURING THE NEGOTIATION

■ ■ ■

Towards agreement

One of the aims in any negotiation is the achievement of a negotiating overlap between the parties. Until one has been achieved, the parties have no prospect of resolving their differences.

Consider a situation where a seller's lowest acceptable price is $50 and the highest price the buyer is willing to pay is only $40. Obviously, the parties are $10 apart.

If that gap cannot be bridged, the parties have no prospect of concluding a deal.

FIGURE 1: THE ABSENCE OF ANY NEGOTIATING OVERLAP

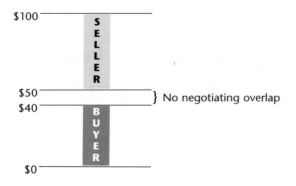

However, in a situation where the seller's lowest acceptable price is $40 and the buyer is prepared to pay up to $50, there is an overlap of $10 in the $40–$50 range.

In this case, (discounting all other factors, of course) the likelihood of doing a deal is extremely high. A range of solutions can be reached within the overlap. In the scenario depicted in Figure 2, the range is somewhere between $40 and $50. The final price reached will depend upon many factors such as supply and demand and the negotiating skill of the respective parties.

FIGURE 2: THE NEGOTIATING OVERLAP

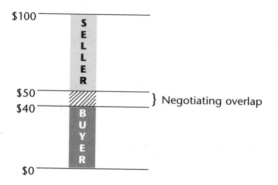

The negotiating overlap is important to bear in mind during any negotiation. It is prudent to ensure that efforts during the negotiations are firstly directed to reaching a position of some degree of overlap. The parties will then be, potentially, in a position to be able to reach an agreement of some kind.

Otherwise, in the absence of any such overlap, all the goodwill, rhetoric and negotiating skill in the world will not be enough to place the parties in a position to be able to reach a deal.

■ ■ ■

Keeping notes

Documenting a situation as it occurs can often be useful. Courts refer to these documents as *contemporaneous notes*.

The vital feature of these notes is that events and conversations are committed to writing either *at the time the events* (they purport to record) occur, *or shortly thereafter*, while the recollection is still fresh in memory.

Courts recognise that human memory fades with time. Particularly, with regard to the fine detail, which can be important when it comes to determining precisely *who said what* in conversations.

This often becomes relevant in contractual disputes, motor vehicle accidents, and in just about any form of litigation.

The courts look very favourably upon contemporaneous notes as an aid to recollecting incidents several years old, particularly as many cases can hinge upon remembering details of crucial conversations.

Case study: Louisville (Ken Tuckey) v Phoenix (Harry Zoner)

How not to keep your notes

Two hypothetical corporations **Louisville Enterprises** and **Phoenix Limited** were involved in a major commercial dispute that ended in litigation.

At the trial, the result of the case hinged upon the truth of certain statements that were said to have been made orally by **Ken Tuckey** (a Director of **Louisville Enterprises**) to **Harry Zoner** (a Director of **Phoenix Limited**).

Ken gave evidence that he kept a contemporaneous diary note of the event and produced it to the court to substantiate his oral evidence.

This ultimately caused **Ken** more harm than good.

Through the evidence of forensic document experts, the judge found that **Ken** had gone back to the original diary entry (probably just before the hearing) and added comments consistent with the version of events that supported his case.

> The court took a very dim view of **Ken's** efforts to "bolster" his evidence by inserting a later entry in the diary and trying to pass it off as a contemporaneous note.
>
> The attempt backfired, and his company **Louisville Enterprises** lost the case.

Properly kept notes can mean the difference between winning and losing a case. At the very least, they can give you negotiating strength on many of the details.

Many of the same reasons to retain successive drafts of an agreement apply to contemporaneous notes. See the section on **Dating and retaining drafts** in Chapter 10.

Golden Rule

Courts recognise that human memory fades over time. Always keep notes.

The palest ink is far better than the best memory.

■ ■ ■

Making concessions

The manner in which a concession is made can often make the concession seem worth more than it is worth. That is, the way in which you make a concession can have a considerable impact upon its perceived value.

For example, if your response to a statement seeking a concession is simply to respond with:

Done!

the recipient of the concession will not place a high value on something obtained and given so freely.

Consider instead, if the process was a little more hard-fought (without overdoing it) and the person seeking the concession was told a little more about how much it would cost to give such a concession and how difficult it would be to do so. By the time the point was actually conceded, it will have gained in value and would more likely be seen to have been a worthwhile win.

In order to be able to grant concessions, you must start from a point much higher than that at which you expect to finish.

This will give you the room you need to work downwards in the give-and-take negotiating environment. Therefore, if you want to sell your house for $100,000, you must list it for sale at a higher figure. As such a pricing structure is an expectation in most negotiations, you will find that if you list the house for sale at $100,000 it is more likely to sell for less than that sum.

A person is more likely to walk away from someone who sets a fair price and sticks to it than from someone who inflates the price and then concedes a little. The person who refuses to concede will be mostly seen as aggressive and unreasonable.

Fewer persons will tend to be upset by a person who "bumps up" the price then "gives a little". A person will walk away from a negotiation with a positive feeling if they feel as if the other side has conceded some ground to them.

A ploy to be aware of is the "vanishing concession", dealt with in the next chapter.

■ ■ ■

Misleading or deceptive conduct

In Australia, whenever a contract dispute arises, Section 52 of the *Trade Practices Act* (concerning misleading or deceptive conduct) is inevitably considered and often claimed.

Section 52 provides that:

A corporation shall not, in trade or commerce, engage in conduct that is misleading or deceptive or is likely to mislead or deceive.

When negotiating the contract, therefore, negotiators must pay careful attention not to do or say anything that can later be claimed to have been misleading or deceptive conduct.

This can even be something as simple as a throwaway line or an anecdote used to illustrate a point. Great care must be exercised to ensure that someone does not subsequently claim that the statement you made was a representation or warranty upon which they later relied and/or which induced them to enter into the transaction.

Section 52 is not intended to change the cut-and-thrust and traditional secrecy of the bargaining process. One is not expected to divulge one's position and to "lay all cards on the table". However, on the other hand, the bargaining process is not to be viewed as a licence to deceive. So, if a party had no intention of contracting on the terms being negotiated (having some other ulterior purpose in mind), then such conduct could be viewed by a court as being misleading.

Whilst you are entitled to bargain hard and be a tough negotiator, it almost goes without saying, that you should refrain from making any untrue or false statement. In the heat of the moment or when one is in "sales mode", one might be tempted to think that exaggerated claims are to be expected from someone trying to make a sale. However, the ramifications could potentially extend beyond simply shrugging it off with a statement such as *caveat emptor* (let the buyer beware).

This is yet another reason why the keeping of detailed notes and/or minutes of the progress of any discussions over the fundamental deal points is continually emphasised in this chapter — especially where such discussions and statements either concern:

- representations or warranties made or given by a party; and/or
- representations or warranties sought by the other party.

Misleading or deceptive conduct can apply to statements made about an existing fact or a prediction made about a future event or happening.

Most importantly, it must be noted that misleading or deceptive conduct can also apply to *silence*. Some might be tempted to think that if they refrain from openly making an untrue statement about something, they can escape any potential liability. This is not always correct.

Courts have held that in situations where there is a duty to disclose a relevant fact or matter, the failure to make such disclosure may constitute misleading or deceptive conduct. The reason being that the aggrieved party in that situation would be entitled to infer from the silence that no danger or detriment existed.

Consider the sale of a restaurant, whose seating arrangements exceeded the limit set by the regulations. The vendor's agent made statements to the purchaser to the effect that the limitations upon the seating capacity were less restrictive than was in fact the case. Also, the manner in which the business was being conducted, supported the impression given to the purchaser. The vendor kept silent on the fact. Even though the purchaser could have discovered, by due enquiry, that the over-seating was a breach, the vendor's failure to disclose the fact, rendered the vendor liable, in those circumstances.

Note that the *intent* of the parties bears no relevance to a court in determining whether a statement or conduct was misleading or deceptive or *likely* to mislead or deceive.

The question is not whether the a person *was* deceived but whether the conduct was misleading or deceptive

Once a party is able to prove:

- there was misleading or deceptive conduct; and

- it suffered loss or damage as a result,

that party has proved its case sufficiently.

A determination by a court of whether the conduct complained of was in fact misleading or deceptive, is a question of fact to be determined in each individual case.

Note also that the operation of the provisions of the *Trade Practices Act* in Australia are mandatory and cannot be excluded by any contract or other disclaimer.

It is important to note that the concept of misleading or deceptive conduct features in a number of other jurisdictions, usually enshrined in fair-trading or unfair competition legislation.

Also, the provisions of section 52 of the Australian *Trade Practices Act* extend to:

the engaging in conduct outside Australia by bodies corporate incorporated or carrying on business within Australia or by Australian citizens or persons ordinarily resident within Australia.

Chapter 7

NEGOTIATING PLOYS — ATTEMPTING TO GAIN THE UPPER HAND

■ ■ ■

Theatrics

Usually, the best answer to theatrics is to recognise the ploy for what it is and "get on with the business at hand".

Theatrical behaviour is to be expected during negotiations. The feigned affront or amazement when you nominate your price, can all be part of the game.

Sometimes, fists hammer the table and booming voices demand:

Are you really serious about doing this deal?!

These situations can sometimes be "manufactured" in an attempt to intimidate you or just to gauge your reaction. If you detect that this is the case, you should resist the natural inclination to want to "hit back". This is when you are most likely to commit an error, or make a rash decision you will later regret.

A raised voice doesn't necessarily demonstrate strength: it is usually a sign of quite the opposite. Genuinely strong or powerful people rarely need to raise their voices or resort to histrionics.

Golden Rule

The key is to not allow yourself to become emotional in any negotiation.

This is sometimes extremely difficult, but it can be practised and learned. Much depends upon your own personality style. Even though the outcome may be personal to you, your emotions will not assist your negotiating abilities or aid your objectivity. Although in some rare circumstances it may be beneficial to show emotion, it is important to generally not show emotion during a negotiation.

Emotions not kept under proper control, often interfere with rational thought processes.

On the other hand, instead of being cleverly theatrical, the person yelling during a negotiation, might only be doing so because of their poorly-developed people skills or exceedingly bad manners.

Being well attuned to the situation (as well as possessing a modicum of people skills yourself) will help you more clearly differentiate between these character traits.

■■■

Seating arrangements

The practice of carefully planning the placement of the "home team" so that they occupy the "head of the table" positions or placing the opposition with their backs to the doors (which is regarded as bad feng-shui), are not the professional practices of negotiations in the 21st century.

To avoid such one-upmanship, many professional negotiators favour the use of round tables. They also hold meetings at a neutral venue.

One recalls (more with amusement, than anything else) the fabled practice of former US president Lyndon Johnson of having installed a special chair — equipped with a hydraulic lift —

into the presidential jet, Air Force One. This was done to ensure that everyone seated in the conference room would have to look up to him.

■■■

Good cop/bad cop

The good cop/bad cop scenario occurs when, in a team of two or more, one person plays the role of a tough and uncompromising person (the "bad cop"), another person plays the role of the "good cop". The good cop tends to adopt a softer approach, sometimes even arguing with the bad cop to appear more reasonable and approachable to the other side. The idea is to win the trust of the other side.

No matter how convincingly the roles are played and how alluring the figure of the good cop might be, it is important to remember that the good cop and the bad cop are on the same side as one another; they are playing a "tag team" match, with the same objectives.

Lawyers are often used in a negotiation to play the part of the "bad cop" on difficult issues. This can be achieved by having the lawyer raise strenuous objections over a particular point — thus paving the way for the manager to "intervene" and "reel the lawyer in" — adding to the perception of the manager's prestige and power, as well as allowing the manager to play the good guy.

■ ■ ■

The flinch

The flinch is one of the oldest tricks in the book, but still effective on the appropriate occasion.

The flinch consists of visibly recoiling and grimacing slightly, as if in pain, upon a suggestion being made by the other side, with which you disagree.

For example, if the other side says:

We'd expect your price to be no more than $10 per unit,

you might recoil, as if in shock, at the suggestion and exclaim in return:

$10 per unit!?

Then say nothing.

In order to be effective, the flinch relies heavily upon the ensuing silence created by the person flinching. Otherwise, if you continue talking, you lose or minimise the effect of the flinch upon the other party and you could end up arguing against yourself.

Conversely, as a purchaser, you may also use the flinch if you have just been quoted a price of $12 per unit. In this case you would recoil in shock and exclaim:

$12 per unit?!

Again, it is often most effective to say nothing more at this point and wait for the other side's response. If you absolutely must say *something* after recoiling at the quoted price, you should limit yourself to:

You'll have to do better than that ...

then STOP and wait for the other side to respond — no matter how lengthy the silence.

■ ■ ■

Nibbling or "just one other thing ..."

Nibbling is a tactic used at the last minute or closing stages of a deal. The argument accompanying the tactic is:

We've come such a long way and agreed on so many major issues, we're not going to let such a minor issue stop us from doing the deal.

In Chapter 8 you will see the tactic used by a car salesman in the case study.

The best form of defence is a recognition of the ploy, with the response that:

We have covered a lot of ground. You have had a long time to raise this issue. I am sure there is a reason why you have left it to the last minute. However, it is too late to now be raising any new issues.

If you're feeling really adventurous, you might wish to add:

If you really feel that strongly about it, I am sure we can discuss it. Naturally, you should have no objection to also dealing with a couple of other issues that we feel should be re-addressed.

If the other party realises there is a price to pay for nibbling (by being "reverse-nibbled") they may withdraw their request, unless it is a genuinely important issue.

In any event, the "reverse-nibble" can operate as a useful "filter" in determining whether the other party's request is genuinely a serious one.

■ ■ ■

The vanishing concession

This occurs where a party ostensibly makes, what appears to be a concession, at the beginning of or during the negotiations. In return, they extract from you an equal or greater concession. Further along the negotiations, they resile from and take back their earlier concession. Worse still, they may even retreat to a position much less favourable than the commencing one.

The reason given, is usually something along the lines of:

The board won't give its approval [to grant the concession].

OR

The time limit has expired.

OR

My boss won't allow me to give it because it is way too much.

You are thereby placed in a much less favourable position than when you commenced negotiations, as you have literally made a "free" concession to the other side. You are then forced to negotiate further (and to often make additional concessions), in order to return the other side to their original position. Meanwhile, the concession you originally made "in return" for theirs (together with any others), invariably stands.

Finally, in what is made to seem like a grand concessionary gesture on their part, they may finally agree (again) to make their original concession.

In this scenario, you are placed in the position of bargaining against yourself and gradually diminishing your own position, at no cost to the other side.

Unethical motor vehicle dealers, advertising special deals, have traditionally employed the tactic. This happens when a prospective customer asks about a deal and is then told that the time limit on the special deal has "lapsed". The tactic is either used as part of a *bait and switch* operation (to lure the customer into a more expensive model) or simply as a huge bargaining lever against the prospective customer.

The tactic is somewhat akin to splitting the difference more than once. See the case study in the next section.

■ ■ ■

Splitting the difference

Splitting the difference is an often-used method of negotiating or resolving a bargaining deadlock. The temptation to use the method is often overwhelming because it is an "easy way out".

The rationale behind the method is that it is "fair" because both parties have conceded an equal amount.

In reality, however, this is an illusion. Whether the process is really "fair" is entirely dependent upon the opening negotiating positions of the respective parties. If one party's position is over-inflated to begin with, then it is not fair.

The argument of fairness is so simple:

You concede X amount and I will do the same
that it can sometimes be irresistible. Particularly so, when there are a final few points left to resolve at the end of a long and hard fought negotiation.

Splitting the difference can often be a trap. When confronted with this, you should look behind the "logic" of the argument, and ascertain whether the other side would have had to make the concession in any event as their opening position was way too high in the first place. In which case, your concession is worth far more and you are, therefore, not trading concessions of equal value.

Case study: splitting the difference — not what it seems

Beware of being asked to split the difference more than once.

Jerry Attrick is a supplier of specialised aged care equipment. **Jerry** is negotiating a supply contract with **Con Artzt**, the CEO of a chain of prestigious private hospitals.

The sole issue left on the table is price.

Jerry's position is that his company is willing to fulfil the contract at a price of $60 million. **Con** states that his company is unwilling to pay more than $40 million.

At **Con's** suggestion, they eventually decide to split the difference. This mutual concession brings the price down to $50 million.

After much further discussion and for various reasons that **Con** explains at length, **Con** returns to his original position of $40 million. **Jerry**, of course, is now at $50 million.

After a long and drawn out negotiating session, **Con** invites **Jerry** to split the difference once more (being the difference between $40 million and $50 million), portraying this as the "fairest" way to resolve the deadlock between them.

By splitting the difference again, an agreement is finally reached by the parties at $45 million.

By splitting the difference twice, **Jerry** has conceded a full $15 million from his original position, whilst **Con** has conceded only $5 million.

To place that into perspective:

- **Jerry's** concession was 75%, while
- **Con** has only had to concede 25%.

Does that seem fair to you?

Golden Rule

One of the more effective ways of avoiding the temptation of splitting the difference, is to deal in values not easily divisible by two.

It is far easier to split a difference of 10 than it is if the difference were, say, a figure of 10.7.

■■■

Silence

Silence can, indeed, be an extremely effective weapon against inexperienced negotiators. It is human nature to want to fill any long silent gaps in a conversation.

Whilst it might seem like a trick to the uninitiated, it is really nothing more than a listening skill.

An experienced negotiator, when confronted by a question or point they would rather not respond to will simply sit in silence. An inexperienced negotiator, more often than not, will feel tempted to break the silence by perhaps attempting to answer their own question or even changing the topic.

Silence tempts the inexperienced to offer more information.

Journalists are taught that silence is an extremely powerful interviewing tool, and that a person being interviewed will tend to fill in silent gaps by volunteering more information than they may have originally intended.

In courtrooms, cross examiners can use silence to lure a witness into offering more information than the witness might have otherwise wished to offer, had they simply been speaking freely.

You need to be aware of this fact and also of your reaction to such silences.

It is interesting to watch experienced negotiators attempting to use silence on one another. Watching a table surrounded by people in silence for five, or ten minutes or more can be quite nerve-racking. Five minutes is an extremely l-o-n-g period of silence to endure in a group. If you have never tried it, you will feel as if you are about to "explode" after as little as one minute.

■ ■ ■

Reluctance

Wanting something too much in a negotiation can be highly detrimental to your cause if you are unable to conceal such a desperate need. If your negotiating counterpart senses that you might be desperate to do the deal at any price, your bargaining power will considerably lessen.

Desperation and eagerness will become apparent, if not kept under conscious control. Poker players know this well and know how to study the signs: body language, expressions and attitudes.

Often, it is the party that cares least about the outcome (the one that is prepared to walk away) that gets the best deal. It is for that reason that many professional negotiators feign reluctance to some degree.

The key is, of course, not to overdo it. Otherwise, one risks being asked:

Well, if you are really not interested in dealing with us, what are you doing here wasting our time?

■ ■ ■

Dealing with such ploys

What is the best position to adopt when a ploy is being over-used and is detrimentally affecting or dramatically slowing the negotiation process?

For example, when the good-cop/bad-cop gambit is being *over-used* on you, the best strategy — in most circumstances — is to politely draw attention to it and suggest that a mutually acceptable resolution is more likely to be achieved, if the parties devote their full attention to the issues in a logical manner (rather than playing games).

When confronted by a flinch, the best move is to simply and calmly restate your position and say nothing more — then wait for a response from the other side.

When faced with a contrived and obviously unacceptable seating arrangement, simply state that the venue in its present form is not acceptable. It is best not to commence the negotiations at all if you feel strongly that the environment is genuinely a hindrance to you and not conducive to a productive negotiation. Otherwise, laugh it off and get down to business.

Awareness of the use of any of these ploys, is usually sufficient for the behaviour to cease. For their effectiveness, many negotiating ploys depend upon the other party being unaware of their use.

Sometimes, a subtle acknowledgment might be all that is necessary to have the practice desist.

If it is not, and if it is appropriate in the circumstances to do so, then a more forceful approach might be required. One should put the other side on notice that their behaviour is seriously threatening the continuation of the negotiations and call for such behaviour to immediately cease and for the parties to focus on resolving the issues in a constructive manner.

If you are aware of a ploy being used against you, you should not fall into the trap of giving the expected response to play their game. The success of any ploy used against you, requires your participation in the "game". If, during the negotiation, someone blusters at you something along the following lines:

Your demands are totally unreasonable!

If the objective of blurting out such a statement is to cause you to lose your cool and to raise the temperature in the room, your "required" response would be something like:

You think we're being unreasonable, what about you? You're the ones being unreasonable ...

Whereas, the situation would be completely defused by not playing the "game" and instead producing the unexpected (and calm) response:

I'm surprised you would say that. But I'd be interested to learn why it is that you have that view.

Where a situation is about to "overheat", being calm and taking the wind out of your attacker's sails is, generally, the best thing you can do, in order to keep the negotiation on track. In the face of any ploy, it is wise to keep sight of the reason the parties are actually negotiating.

On the other hand, if things have degenerated into a virtual brawl and you see no point continuing with the session, you can send a very powerful message (where appropriate to do so) by simply packing your briefcase and quietly leaving the room.

Chapter 8

NEGOTIATING MYTHS — THE THINGS SOME PEOPLE FALL FOR ...

■ ■ ■

"The pot is empty"

The pot is empty ploy is a slight variation on the flinch, that involves the complete absence of bargaining and counter-offers. It is sometimes also referred to as the *Mother Hubbard* tactic — "the cupboard is bare".

Upon hearing the other side's price the standard response is limited to either:

You'll have to improve on that.

OR

We can't afford that much.

The suggestion is that the (money) "pot is empty" and there is no more money available to pay such a high asking price. The whole idea is to get the other side to start bargaining against themselves.

If the other side indeed responds by taking the bait and making a concession in response to the "pot is empty", the process is continually repeated until the other side stops making any more concessions. By that stage, you will be better placed to assess whether that is in fact their absolute lowest price.

Of course, the obvious response to counter "the pot is empty" is to ask:

How much better do we need to do before we can do business?

OR

What price did you have in mind?

The main caveat here is that once you start to bargain against yourself, you will be "on the run" and will have surrendered total control of the negotiation. When this happens, a good negotiator on the other side will then seek to capitalise upon their advantage by placing you under more and continual pressure to keep making further concessions, until arriving at your bottom-line price.

This sustains and maintains their advantage, as this is the most prized piece of information that every negotiator can know about the other side's position.

This is the main reason that every motor-car dealer will always ask you how much you want for your trade-in vehicle and how much you wish to pay for the new vehicle. They already know *their own* bottom-line positions on both. In this manner, they also find out *yours* and thereby maintain total control of the negotiation. The entire time, you *never ever* know their bottom-line position. This applies more so when you've been well and truly "fleeced", since they still want you to feel good about your purchase.

This leads to another important point:

Golden Rule

Never gloat about a negotiation victory or boast about how you settled way above your bottom line.

Besides being "tacky" and unprofessional, it severely erodes your credibility in future negotiations and tends to operate as a great inspiration for the other side to seek ways and methods of repaying your bravado.

■ ■ ■

"The offer is good for today only"

Genuine offers are generally able to withstand the test of time; that is, it will indeed be rare that an offer made today could not remain open until tomorrow, in order to allow you sufficient time to consider it.

Consider your average car salesman. You will meet him in our case study (entitled **but everyone signs it!**) a little further on. He has you in his dealership and you are ready to buy. The salesman will do everything within his power to have you sign up for a deal there and then. Once you leave, you then have the power of comparison shopping. A good salesman will do all he can to overcome any objections to you making a buying decision on the spot.

He will more than likely consult his "sales manager" and make, what he tells you is, the offer of a lifetime. Now comes the crunch ...

The offer is good for today only.

OR

The offer stands until you walk out of here.

This is all designed to place pressure upon you to accept their offer, rather than to "risk" getting a less attractive deal elsewhere. The pressure comes from the fact that you are made to feel that you will only find a less attractive deal elsewhere — but that you won't have the chance to come back and get this "great" deal again.

It will be a rare occasion that such a ploy is actually genuine. You need to be thoroughly satisfied (preferably by independent verification) that the offer is indeed a great one and must be acted upon immediately, in order to secure it.

One response is to ask *Why?*

The answer should provide some valuable clues to help assess whether the deadline is a ploy or genuine.

Another way might be to say:

It sounds like a good deal. If it is as good as you say then you won't mind me [EITHER] *comparing it with* [X] [OR] *talking it over with my* [boss, spouse or other higher authority]. *I can get back to you with an answer by midday tomorrow.*

Usually, a sensible party to a negotiation will allow you to go away and independently verify that the deal is good and to just "think it over". This is especially so where that party genuinely believes that the deal is exceptional and that you will not be able to do better elsewhere. It is more impressive when they are prepared to give the opportunity to independently verify the fact:

Sure, go and check for yourself.

However, even in such an event, it would be unreasonable to expect an unlimited timeframe to be able to do so.

In the car sales example above, it might indeed be fair for you to be asked to provide an answer by, say, "lunchtime tomorrow". However, remember that all sales training is designed to get you to make the buying decision "now", rather than to have provide you with the opportunity of yourself or others dissuading you from the buying decision.

■ ■ ■

"Take it … or else"

This is a variation on the "offer is good for today only" ploy, but is designed to have the same effect upon you; to accelerate your decision.

I have another guy interested, who is coming back [or calling me back] in an hour. I don't think it will still be around after that.

OR

Unless you buy today, the special factory rebate expires. You will then have to pay full price.

This ploy creates the urgency within you by clearly showing you what will happen if you fail or delay the buying decision; someone else will buy it or you will miss the deadline on the special rebate.

Moving away from the car-buying example, the ploy might look like:

If you don't agree to our terms today and settle this, we will sue.

OR

If we don't strike a deal now, we will go and do the deal with Party X [for added effect, Party X might be your fiercest competitor].

■ ■ ■

The "standard" form

I don't know how many times, during contract negotiations, I have heard the mantra:

We can't change the wording of the document. It's a standard form.

This is one of the "oldest tricks in the book". One must understand that there is *no* such thing as a "standard" and inviolable form — even if there was such a thing, there would be no requirement to have to accept it "as is".

As the saying goes: *everything is negotiable.*

Unfortunately, some people are intimidated into accepting a "standard form", often without challenge or compromise.

Such intimidation — designed to place pressure upon you to sign the document without change — can be applied in quite a logical-sounding and gentlemanly manner, without any overt aggression. For this reason, it can be a formidable weapon.

The "intimidator" will achieve this by making statements designed to make you feel that *you* are the one being unreasonable in your request. The "intimidator" will recount how the document has been "approved" by a brace of leading Queens Counsel and has been accepted, without question, by some of the largest companies in the country. The logical inference being:

> *If there really was something that needed changing, the intellectual might of all those companies' law firms or legal departments would have surely detected any deficiency by now.*

Another technique used, is to suggest that your proposed amendments are already addressed by the present wording of the document. To legitimise the assertion, it could be supported by a statement along the following lines:

> *We have a Queens Counsel's opinion confirming that.*

Looking behind such a statement, one should immediately realise that a Queens Counsel's opinion (regardless of how impressive or famous the author) is, in fact, only an *opinion* on the law. The opinion itself is not the statement of the law. It is a subjective interpretation of the application of the existing law to a particular set of circumstances. Think about it — when eminent Queens Counsel, representing opposing parties, engage in litigation, one of them must lose. Every day Queens Counsel lose cases! They cannot *always* be right.

When confronted by such a statement, a useful response to the "intimidator" can sometimes be:

> *If you can refer us to any **High Court decisions**, which have ruled that the document in its present form would be interpreted in our favour, then we would be happy to reconsider our position. However, we have no wish to become the first test-case that rules against us and proves you wrong.*

As an aside, if you were so bold as to actually request a copy of the opinion (out of pure interest), you would probably be told that it was privileged, was difficult to obtain, or, could only be shown if you agreed to contribute to its cost!

A technique taught in sales is that a statement is more credible if it appears in writing. That is why most sales presentations have a presentation folder or slides to repeat and reinforce — in writing — important statements that are communicated verbally.

Another place you are likely to see the power of the written statement is in hotels. Often, the hotel policy on "check-out time by 10 o'clock" is stated in writing. By the way, there probably isn't a hotel that would not extend its check-out time, if you asked. Since hotels adopted the practice of communicating the check-out time to guests in writing, fewer people have asked for extended check-out times.

Case study:
but, everyone signs it!

Think back to the last time you purchased a car. Sitting at the dealer's desk you were presented with the "standard form" contract to sign.

When you asked to make amendments to the form, you were told that it could not be done because it was a *standard form*.

Many who hear such a statement, will accept that a standard form is one that cannot be questioned or changed.

To further increase the legitimacy of the document, you might even have been told that it was even approved by the World Motor Vehicle & Transport Association (or some similar impressively-named body) — the statement obviously designed to convey the inference: *Who are* you *to question the might and wisdom of such an organisation?*

The salesperson would often add: *Everyone signs them* (without question or complaint).

The statement being meant to suggest that your request was quite an unusual and unreasonable one. (The chances were quite high that the salesperson had never actually even read the standard form and did not understand — let alone be in any position to be able to negotiate — its contents with you.)

At this point, if you were still not convinced, you might have been told:

We've never had a problem in 20 years of doing business

OR EVEN

> *We have sold many cars to lawyers, none of whom have ever questioned the form.*
>
> Chances were that the salesperson had not actually been at the dealership for any great length of time to be able to make such a statement with any authority or degree of credibility.
>
> Of course, accepting any of those statements is always at your peril.

A final word on standard forms. If you absolutely cannot persuade another party to vary or amend its standard form, there may be another way; this most frequently occurs in the area of information technology (IT) contracts — where the parent company has settled the form of the licensing agreement and usually does not grant its subsidiaries the right to amend the form itself.

In such cases, however, many companies will agree to a secondary amending agreement to take into account local laws, market conditions and practices.

Such an amending agreement must be carefully worded and usually provides for the acceptance of the terms in the primary licensing document except for the following changes, which are then listed.

The amending agreement will then usually set forth the amended conditions that will either replace or supplement those in the original standard form. You should ensure that you consult a lawyer to properly and carefully draft any such amending agreement.

Battle of the forms

If you have agreed on the fundamental commercial terms of the deal such as price, description of the goods, delivery date, etc, there is a way of "fighting fire with fire" against the "standard form" gambit.

Beware, that if you accept the offer and ignore or fail to mention your non-acceptance of the whole or part of the standard form, you may be taken to have accepted their terms.

A more effective way to "accept" the other party's offer, might be by using *your* company's standard terms in your response to the other party's offer. Provided, of course, that your company's standard terms contain a term along the following lines (and most properly drafted documents will do so):

These terms and conditions shall apply to the contract. Any other terms, conditions and representations made whether oral or in writing and not appearing herein are hereby expressly excluded and superseded.

This, of course, is not strictly an acceptance of the offer. At law, this action constitutes a rejection of the other party's standard terms and is actually a counter-offer made by your company on its own standard terms.

If the other party proceeds on the basis of your response, they will have — by their actions — accepted your terms. This is the so-called "battle of the forms".

Golden Rule

There is no such thing as a standard form that cannot be changed, as circumstances require. As with any agreement, changes are made by negotiation.

Recognise the "standard form" ploy as simply a negotiating tactic.

■ ■ ■

"Legal won't approve any changes"

This is simply another variation of the "standard form" ploy.

It works on the "higher authority" negotiating principle. It often goes something like this:

> *I'd really like to help you out with this, but my hands are tied.*

OR

> *My legal department just won't allow me to change this.*

You are expected to believe that an all-powerful and all-knowing authority exists within the company, called the legal department. This supernatural authority supposedly has the final say in all contractual matters.

That, of course, is total nonsense.

Lawyers may have the final say on *legal* matters. However, some decisions are *commercial* matters for the relevant manager to ultimately decide upon. In some situations, a manager may seek legal advice. Remember, however, that advice is just that: *advice*. It is not an inviolable order or direction that must be followed.

Remember that managers run companies, not lawyers. **Ultimately, managers make the decisions**. Many managers ignore legal advice every day of the week (sometimes at their peril) for a variety of commercial considerations. Often, it is for no other reason than for the sake of doing the deal.

Therefore, if there is a good commercial reason for changing a term in a document, the "legal won't approve it" argument should never be accepted at face value.

However, assuming the company you are dealing with is one of those rare (and enlightened!) companies in which lawyers have an extremely high degree of influence, the best way is to actually communicate the required changes and amendments to the lawyers for their consideration.

Don't let the person with whom you are dealing assume the role of "gatekeeper" by pre-empting the lawyer's decision to automatically veto whatever it is you require.

Most lawyers will listen to and consider cogent and coherent commercial arguments, before giving their advice. All lawyers must only act on instructions. Lawyers in legal departments of corporations must also *always* take instructions from their client. The client in such a case will just happen to be the manager in charge of the project or department with which you are dealing.

So if you pursue the matter on a *commercial basis* rather than a *legal basis*, you have a much-improved chance of achieving a favourable result.

Golden Rule

Managers make decisions in companies, not lawyers.

Managers have the discretion to overrule any legal advice on commercial considerations.

Recognise the "legal won't approve it" ploy as simply a negotiating tactic.

■ ■ ■

"Don't worry, we'd never enforce that one"

You are most likely to hear the above statement uttered after making an objection to an unfavourable or unfair clause in a contract.

It defies belief that anyone (who might be otherwise sane and sensible) could ever fall for this.

What is more amazing that an apparently intelligent senior manager could ever sit at a negotiating table and seriously say that their company would never enforce a particular provision of the contract. However, I have actually had such a statement made to me (in all seriousness) by an opposing lawyer during a negotiation!! Mercifully, most lawyers do know better.

The statement ranks highly among those deliberately calculated to insult one's intelligence.

It demands the obvious response:

Well if you do not intend to enforce it, you will have no objection to taking it out.

If the response you receive to such a request is:

No, I can't delete this, however...

this should be your signal to run, in the opposite direction.

There is no sensible or reasonable rationalisation for the *we'd never enforce that one* ploy. The only motives that could possibly be ascribed to anyone making such a statement are either:

1) sinister and devious; or

2) plain ignorance and abject stupidity.

If the particular clause that you find objectionable stays in the contract, it is "live" and completely enforceable against you, despite any statements made in negotiations.

This is precisely the reason most contracts contain a boilerplate clause to the effect that the contract includes all of the terms agreed between the parties and expressly excludes any statements or representations made unless they are recorded in writing within that contract document (see **entire agreement clause** for a further explanation in the **Use of extrinsic evidence** section in Chapter 12).

A more subtle way of dealing with the issue might be:

We understand your assurance, but what if, for some reason, none of us are around when the time comes? You will appreciate that this type of situation will need to be properly documented for the benefit and security of each party to the agreement. This will avoid any misunderstandings. We will require your company to actually translate such an assurance into positive action to give us the appropriate level of comfort that it would in fact never prejudice us.

The advice we have received on the most effective way to achieve this, is to simply delete the offending portion of the clause. If your company is serious about its assurance, there should be no difficulty in providing us with that comfort. You would not be surrendering any rights since you have already stated categorically that your company never intends to enforce the clause.

Golden Rule

Any clause in a contract is "live" and completely enforceable against you, despite any verbal assurance to the contrary.

■ ■ ■

"It's just a formality"

This is another one of those variations on the "the contract doesn't really matter" routine.

A contract whether in business or personally, is never "just" a formality. It is a serious and enduring endeavour.

Your signature on the document constitutes *your reputation on the line* and under scrutiny. It can either gain you recognition for your astuteness or, at worst, be a lasting testament to incompetence.

Remember, once you sign it, it *all* counts.

When it comes to contracts, undoing a single minute of absent-mindedness or stupidity can often take years in the courts and cost many hundreds of thousands of dollars.

More importantly, your reputation — as a person who can be trusted to safeguard the corporation's interests in such matters — may never fully recover.

In some jurisdictions, to even have the remotest possibility of undoing harsh and unconscionable contracts (especially in a commercial context) will usually require an admission that the company's officers did not understand what they were doing and that the company was in an unequal bargaining position (simply being dumb or out-negotiated doesn't satisfy that requirement).

Such admissions will only come at great personal embarrassment to those involved. Even so, there is no guarantee that they will be successful in undoing an executive's costly mistakes.

Case study: cross-examination of an executive

In court, the executive would probably go through something like the following exchange under cross-examination. You can almost hear it:

Q: You have been a manager for how many years?
A: Over 20 years.

Q: Over those 20 years, you have encountered many important documents?

A: Yes.

Q: Is it safe to say that your employer regards you as a competent and careful businessperson?

A: Yes.

Q: When you encounter an important document, is it your normal practice to exercise care in reading such a document?

A: Yes.

Q: If there was something that you did not understand, you would have had it clarified before signing it?

A: Yes.

Q: Your company regularly uses the XYZ law firm does it not?

A: Yes.

Q: As an experienced and well-regarded businessperson, you understand the nature of signing a contract and its implications?

A: Yes.

Q: You have said that is your practice to check things before signing your name to them?

A: Yes.

Q: You knew this was an important document didn't you?

A: Yes.

By this point, the executive under cross-examination is forced to admit that he/she did not exercise care on the occasion and that it was his/her failure that allowed the error to finally slip through.

Such an admission may be enough to, quite literally, end an executive's career.

In most jurisdictions, unfair contracts legislation is usually focused on rectifying consumer claims or "David and Goliath" claims. These are claims made by smaller companies against large Fortune 500 companies, that have unfairly exercised their superior bargaining power and position over a smaller company.

Except in unusual circumstances, courts are reluctant to intervene in commercial situations where the parties were in a position to obtain proper advice and simply exercised a choice not to do so. Courts will not, as a general rule, intervene to correct commercial laziness, incompetence or stupidity.

Golden Rule

Signed contracts always count.

Your signature on the document can and will be used against you when necessary.

Chapter 9

FROM NEGOTIATIONS TO CONTRACT

■ ■ ■

In the sometimes-frantic pace of deal-making in business, where an executive may often be working on two or more deals at any one time, the pressure of getting things accomplished quickly often creates an irresistible temptation to find short-cuts.

This can sometimes manifest itself in a failure to document (or properly document) a deal or transaction.

As the parties develop a certain rapport during the (often arduous) negotiation process, a higher-than-usual level of trust may be assumed of the other party. This is usually despite the fact that the people negotiating the deal will not be the ones fulfilling its terms, over the duration of the contract. Also, many contracts entered into tend to "outlive" the parties who originally put the deal together, as people are either promoted within a company or simply change jobs.

For these reasons, we will undertake a closer examination of the rationale for having written contracts in all transactions.

■ ■ ■

Why a handshake isn't worth the paper it's (not) written on

Handshake deals tend to arise because of the personalities of the parties involved or the circumstances of the deal.

It is rare for a major deal to be entirely consummated by a handshake without there first having been an exchange of emails, letters, specifications or other documents between the parties or their representatives.

There are a number of stories of handshake deals gone wrong; however, the standout example has to be the US oil company that received a damages award of over $10 billion when the court upheld a handshake deal, over an unsigned piece of paper, as a binding contract.

The problem with handshake deals is often not confined to resolving the question:

Is there a contract between the parties?

More often, the existence of a contract between parties is clear and, instead, the question tends to be:

What are the terms of the agreement between the parties?

This is where matters become more complicated than the parties could have foreseen at the time of their handshake.

Things become awkward when a matter ends up in litigation. A court must assess one person's word against that of another. The contest is reduced to:

We agreed on black,

whilst the other party will typically assert with equal conviction and vigour that:

We agreed on white.

Note that the differences do not necessarily have to be so polarised. A subtle detail or nuance is all that may be necessary to alter the entire flavour of the deal for one of the parties.

Who is telling the truth?

Assessments must be made by a court of one party's character and bona fides. Invariably, someone's name and reputation ends up being forever tarnished; sometimes neither party emerges unscathed.

Remembering that victories, in such an event, can sometimes end as pyrrhic ones. At worst, they can be public relations nightmares, as the tabloid press scramble for every salacious detail of a judge's criticism of the veracity of a particular executive, who has been unfortunate enough to have become embroiled in the controversy.

Sometimes, attempting to simplify matters with a handshake instead of a contract can lead to further and greater complications than those the parties originally wished to avoid.

In the event that an agreement is made without a formal contract, parties should attempt to document, at least the key points of the deal in some way, even if done by a simple letter confirming the deal, after the event. The main points can even be scribbled down onto the proverbial restaurant napkin over lunch. That way, if there is any dispute over the key details, the parties will become immediately aware of the misunderstandings or differences.

It is often the process of reducing an agreement to writing that parties can become aware of subtle (but important) differences in their understanding of the meaning of a key term. Seeing an agreed concept in "black and white" for the first time can have the effect of greatly clarifying one's original understanding of an issue. It is for this reason that a first draft of a document can sometimes trigger the following kinds of responses in your negotiating counterpart in relation to certain key issues (previously though to have been resolved at the negotiating table):

I'm not so sure that's what we really had in mind.

OR

Maybe this isn't going to work the way we first thought it would.

The advice from all of this is that it is better to properly document any deal using the parties' lawyers, and to make that deal effective only when the parties sign the contract.

■ ■ ■

Embodying negotiations into a contract

The ideal aim is for the agreement reached by the parties to be embodied into a **single** document at the end of negotiations; a document that effectively captures and records **all** the terms of the agreement between the parties.

This will include all of the deal terms, the boilerplate clauses, and any schedules or annexures.

In other words, the aim is to achieve a single *stand-alone* document. The stand-alone aspect is important when it comes to certainty of the terms of the deal.

One of the reasons for creating a stand-alone document is to confirm the operation of the *parol evidence rule* (see **Use of extrinsic evidence** in Chapter 12). No one wishes to be surprised by an assertion from "left field" that a key term of the deal was omitted from the contract.

Keep detailed minutes

In complex and drawn out negotiations, a convenient way of keeping track of the key terms under discussion is to keep detailed minutes of the progress of those discussions. Minutes that are freely shared with the other side are much more likely to bring out any misunderstandings at an early stage of proceedings. They could also become a convenient and powerful evidentiary tool in the case of litigation.

Minutes also facilitate the briefing of lawyers, in the event that the lawyers' first introduction to the transaction is after the stage that the "deal terms" have been settled.

Keep a rolling memorandum

Another variation on the approach of using minutes is to use the "rolling memorandum" which documents the terms discussed at each meeting and rolls to the next — accumulating details of agreed points.

In this way, drafting "surprises" and time-consuming renegotiation of settled issues can be avoided when the first draft of the contract is issued to the other party.

Check all clauses, even old ones

Every standard form or boilerplate clause pasted into an agreement must be carefully checked for its applicability to the current transaction. A clause that may have been applicable in the last deal, may not necessarily be so in its current form. Subtle changes may need to be made. All clauses must be carefully checked with this in mind.

Mindless cutting-and-pasting is a sign of inexperience and carelessness.

Another temptation to be avoided is the practice of the one-page "agreement".

Case study: the one-page agreement

A short-cut to drawing contracts

Rather than pay lawyers to draw a contract, wouldn't it be easier to just have a one-page list drawing together and listing all of the correspondence that has passed between the parties during the negotiation?

Such bundles usually consist of a miscellaneous collection of correspondence between the parties and/or other notes, specifications or other documents.

This is often perceived as a "smart" way to have all of the benefits of a written and signed contract with the minimum of effort. Usually, such decisions are based on wishing to save on two things, which are always scarce in any business: time and money.

However, in the long run, such a decision invariably proves to be a false economy.

Why? Because there may be (and often are) inconsistencies between some of the documents.

Some of the correspondence will contain offers and counter-offers of various kinds and usually for different parts of the deal. It therefore, becomes difficult to piece together an accurate picture of the precise terms that the parties actually and finally agreed upon.

How will such inconsistencies be resolved? Which document takes precedence over another? What if there is a dispute, how will it be resolved? What happens with so-called "side-letters"? (Side-letters are supplementary or additional agreements between the parties not incorporated into the primary contract.)

In effect, the parties may be tempted to think they have a completed and properly documented deal, whereas the reality is that they have not. Such a false sense of security often magnifies the parties' surprise in the event of a dispute between them.

This practice of "bundling" is an invitation to litigation, as it throws wide open the possibility for the other party to rely upon an exception to the parol evidence rule.

This means there is much less certainty concerning the precise terms upon which the parties have actually agreed. See **Use of extrinsic evidence** in Chapter 12.

■ ■ ■

The "end" of the negotiations

So you've been involved in weeks (or sometimes even months) of hard-fought negotiations. You've had to make a number of concessions to get this far, but in return, have been able to extract a number of significant concessions from your opponent that will make the deal a winner for your company.

What do some normally do at this point? They breathe a sigh of relief that the negotiations are finally over and that the deal is done.

However, the deal is not yet done. At least, not usually until the final form of contract is agreed upon and executed. Many things can change before that point is reached.

Many, at this point, handover to others the process of committing the terms of the deal to paper. Depending on the size of the company, this could be left to the company's legal department or — at the opposite end of the spectrum — to more junior members of the deal team.

People often think that the hard part is over at the conclusion of the oral negotiations concerning the "deal terms". In fact, once the deal terms have been settled, this is where the real negotiations — those that could cause the greatest impact to the parties — usually begin. These are matters such as indemnity clauses, the treatment of consequential loss, liquidated damages provisions, intellectual property issues, etc.

Even where a major "deal term" — such as the purchase price of a business being sold — has been taken care of, major issues such as the following will remain:

- post-completion price adjustment formulae;
- the precise warranties that will be given;
- dispute resolution processes and mechanisms;
- indemnities;
- the disclosure letter;
- tax warranties; and
- the list goes on.

One further point to take into consideration is your exposure to the process of *nibbling* by the other side. Chapter 7 contains a more detailed explanation of the process. You will also see an example of the tactic, used in the following case study.

Case study: when the negotiation "really" ends

Remember when you last purchased a motor-car?

You finally decided on the make of car to buy, you drove it and talked "turkey" with the salesman. You sat at the salesman's desk negotiating the price of the car for hours. You were subjected to the game of the salesman going back and forth between you and the (sometimes) fictitious sales manager for another minor concession. At the moment you finally agreed on a price and shook the salesman's hand on a deal, you let your guard down. You were overcome with feelings of relief that the process was finally over.

Then you were taken into another office "to just finalise the paperwork".

The environment was congenial and very non-confrontational. You were congratulated on your wise decision to purchase the XYZ motor vehicle. You were given a cup of coffee and there was small talk about how the car was voted "car of the year" — all calculated to give you the ammunition you would later need to reinforce your buying decision. All very friendly.

It is at that point that the dealer is able to substantially increase its profit margin on the deal by slipping in the cost of such items as rustproofing, paint protection, fabric protection or some other accessory. Often, an extra thousand dollars or more can be added to the price of the vehicle with little or no buyer resistance. These are usually accessories carrying huge profit margins.

All this was achieved once you thought the buying process was over.

So it can be with commercial contracts — significant terms of a deal can be sometimes re-written or "slipped in" under your guard after the conclusion of negotiations.

■ ■ ■

Didn't we already agree on that?

It is at this point of the transaction that persons, who may not have been previously involved in the negotiations, often join in. They might be lawyers or other persons to help "write up the deal".

These "new" persons will rely upon the instructions they receive. The different interpretations and focus can strongly influence the wording of clauses. If the instructions are sufficiently poor, the draft agreement's terms may bear little resemblance to the understanding that the parties had when they left the negotiating table.

Lawyers will generally consider and probe into consequences and ramifications that may not have been previously considered during the negotiations. After the conclusion of a negotiation session, and in response to a lawyer's consideration of the broader ramifications, it is not uncommon to hear an executive comment:

That was not discussed.

OR

We never considered that issue.

This broader perspective is often helpful in bringing a higher level view to the transaction and putting all of the potential liability consequences and issues into context, in balancing the risk/reward ratio of the deal.

Also, many of the boilerplate items will rarely have been discussed during the negotiation. The parties will consequently not have information on these items with which to brief the lawyers. As a consequence, the lawyer's precedent document's boilerplate will be the party's first position. Lawyers, wishing to do the best for their clients and safeguard their interests, will usually ensure that such clauses favour their own client's position.

Such *opening* positions, if unchallenged, will end up being *final* positions on a number of significant issues. You need to be aware of this aspect in any negotiation.

Golden Rule

An unscrupulous party may seek to gain an advantage over the other party by "slipping in" a clause at the last minute. It may even be a point that was never previously discussed or negotiated.

Some might be tempted to think that even if something is "slipped-in" under their guard, they can rely on the notes of their negotiations or on copies of the correspondence that passed between the parties, during the course of the negotiations. They *might* be able to, but that could very well mean litigation.

In such a case, one must beware of the impact of the *entire agreement* clause. See the section on **Proofreading** of contracts in Chapter 10.

■■■

"Letter of intent" or "MOU" or "terms sheet"

Letters of intent are preliminary documents usually created to serve as a record of the "headline" deal terms of a transaction. They may sometimes bear any number of different labels such as *memorandum of understanding* (MOU) or *heads of agreement* or even *terms sheet*. These labels are not precise legal terms. The names generally mean what the parties intend them to mean.

Letters of intent are sometimes produced to maintain momentum in a transaction and to attempt to "wed" the parties to continuing discussions that will ultimately progress to a completed transaction.

Often, the letter of intent stage is the point of handover of the transaction to the lawyers and others to deal with the boilerplate clauses and to "finalise the paperwork". For a more information about boilerplate contract clauses, you should consult **Understanding Commonly Used Contract Terms: Boilerplate Clauses**, the fourth title in the *Commercial Contracts for Managers Series*.

The ever-present question behind these documents is:

Are they intended by the parties to be legally binding?

Parties need to be absolutely clear on this point, before committing anything to writing. Such understanding needs to also be *expressly* stated within the document.

There are at least three key areas to consider when preparing such a letter:

- Is the letter designed to merely record terms discussed with NO binding effect upon the parties?

- Is it the intent that there will be no legally binding agreement between the parties *unless and until* the parties have executed a definitive agreement that includes all of the terms and conditions of the transaction?

- Does the letter create any obligation upon the parties to enter into a transaction or to negotiate?

Golden Nugget

"Subject to contract" or "subject to misunderstanding"?

The use of the words *subject to contract* alone, may be insufficient to obtain maximum clarity in a situation.

In a number of jurisdictions, this expression has been held to have one of three different meanings:

1) The parties have reached finality and intend to be bound, but also intend to have the terms restated in a more comprehensive agreement incorporating all of the terms of the deal.

   In this case, there IS a contract between the parties.

2) The parties have agreed on terms, but performance of one or more terms is conditional on execution of a formal agreement.

   In this case, there IS a contract between the parties.

3) The parties do not intend to have a concluded deal, unless and until they execute a formal written agreement.

   In this case, there is NO contract between the parties.

As you can see, the key is to clearly state the parties' intentions. If they do not intend to be bound *unless and until* they execute a formal agreement, then it is wise to expressly say so.

An overriding caution is necessary at this point. Labels are not the be-all-and-end-all of things, at law.

A party's conduct must be consistent with the labels applied, in the contract, to such conduct.

Where parties sign a document stating that the parties "do not intend to be bound" and the parties *act* and *regard themselves* as if they were bound, this will be highly relevant to a court in assessing whether the parties should be bound.

In most jurisdictions, the parties' actions will override the words they have used, in the event of any inconsistency between the two.

To put it another way, it is not possible to paint a wall black and expect it to be regarded as white simply because one has signed a document declaring it to be white.

Chapter 10

DRAWING UP THE NEGOTIATED AGREEMENT

■ ■ ■

Who draws the contracts? Or "who draws wins"

Drafting control in a transaction is something to be aimed for on every occasion.

Why? Notice the use of the word "control". That is what the drafting process can usually provide to you. Having control over the meeting/negotiation agenda also gives you an added ability to influence the outcome of the contract document.

Some are tempted to shy away from the task of producing the first draft; usually for reasons of cost.

They think that the extra amount of money spent on lawyers on such a time-consuming process, is a saving they have immediately generated.

However, this thinking is usually a false economy, in the long run. True, the legal costs may be higher for the drafting party — since contract drafting is usually (but not always) a more time-consuming process than contract reviewing. However, the cost can be a great deal more if the contract is less favourably oriented to that party. Also, if the first draft produced by the other side is so far conceptually wide of the mark, the extra costs in further negotiations and redrafting will often outweigh the initial perceived saving.

In a transaction, the first draft will set the tone and tend to define the limits and boundaries of a deal. Generally, amendments to first drafts of contracts rarely redefine those boundaries. To achieve such a redefinition becomes a much more difficult task, after the issue of the first draft.

Most lawyers will stress the importance of drafting control in a transaction. It is an importance not to be underestimated. The drafting party has the opportunity to largely control the shape and outcome of the final document.

Conversely, some will argue the non-drafting party has the advantage as it has a better "bird's eye view" of the transaction. This arises since they are not preoccupied with the time-consuming task of producing and shaping the document.

More often than not, however, the non-drafting party can do little more than "twiddle its thumbs", while awaiting receipt of the document from the drafting party. Such extra free time can be rarely put to use in securing a better competitive advantage than that of drafting the document, in the first place.

That same "bird's eye view" of the non-drafting party can be obtained within the drafting party's camp, by simply showing the draft document to, say, a senior manager or director (with little or no involvement in the transaction), and eliciting comments.

In some instances, convention dictates which party will produce the first draft:

- in most sale transactions, it will be the vendor;
- in a loan, it will be the lender; and
- in a lease of property, it will be the landlord.

However, the right is sometimes easily given up, out of apathy or ignorance. In this case, persistence pays.

The bargaining strength of the parties can sometimes dictate the order of things.

The drafting party can, in a competitive bid situation, make use of the competitive tension that exists, to extract more favourable concessions and terms in a negotiation. See more about the role of competitive tension in the negotiation process in the **Auction situations** section in Chapter 3.

In any event, you should never allow yourself to be deterred from trying to secure this advantage to your position.

■■■

Marked-up drafts

During the course of negotiations, amendments made to a draft of a contract need to be identified in some convenient way.

There is nothing more frustrating than to receive a fresh draft of a 100 page agreement, where there is no discernable way of identifying the changes made.

To have to laboriously compare the hard copies of two documents side-by-side in this way is wasteful, time-consuming and of no benefit to anyone. It also increases the chances that something might be missed.

The customary way to show changes to a previous version of a document is to *mark-up* the document; sometimes this may be referred to as *redlining* (or *blacklining*).

The name comes from the process of <u>underlining</u> additions to the text and showing any deletions as ~~strikethrough~~ text. Most word processing programmes can perform this process. In some word processing programmes, the amended text appears on-screen coloured red, hence the use of the term *redlining*.

However, one word of warning!

Unscrupulous persons have been known to turn off the redlining feature of the word processing programme, in order to "slip" some changes past you — without detection — then to turn it back on again! In such cases, you need to compare the documents. This can be done physically or (more easily) electronically. One other security method to adopt is to simply take in only the redlined changes into your copy.

If for some reason, marking-up the document is not possible, then the party having made the amendments should be required to, at least, produce a schedule listing all of the changes and their substance.

■ ■ ■

Dating and retaining drafts

All drafts retained should always be dated. Again, most word processing programmes automatically insert these particulars in headers or footers. Do not take it for granted that it will be there; always check for yourself.

Putting aside considerations of storage space, it is generally good practice to keep all successive drafts and mark-ups of a document in a transaction. This enables a clear evolutionary pattern of a document to be traced. This can be a useful tool in helping a court resolve any ambiguity in a clause.

It can also be useful in the event that a party makes assertions over a particular aspect of the deal, which may not be entirely correct. For example, consider where a party asserts that a particular warranty was the subject of intense discussions from the beginning of the transaction. If such a term was only found to have been introduced into the document in (say) the final draft, the claimant's assertion may be considerably undermined.

Such spurious allegations, assertions and claims tend to be made in a defensive capacity when a party is being sued for some breach of contract or other wrongdoing. That is, by adopting the mentality that the best form of defence is attack.

Being able to quickly deflate such claims, gives the other party an advantage either in the courtroom or at the negotiating table. Either way, it is an advantage definitely worth having.

Another pattern that may emerge from a series of drafts is a where particular clause is consistently being added by one party in their mark-up and then deleted by the other party in their own mark-up. This pattern, at least, demonstrates that a point remained contentious over a long period. It becomes much more difficult for a party to argue that it was an issue long since settled, when the document trail shows that it remained a contentious issue for a lengthy period.

One final point. It is a sensible practice to include on the cover sheet of any draft agreement produced wording to the effect:

DRAFT — FOR DISCUSSION PURPOSES ONLY.

OR

DRAFT ISSUED FOR DISCUSSION PURPOSES ONLY. THIS IS NOT INTENDED TO BE A LEGALLY BINDING DOCUMENT.

■ ■ ■

Proofreading

Proofreading is probably the most unglamorous task of them all (or perhaps it might be photocopying). However, the consequences of failing to thoroughly and properly proofread documents, prior to executing them, can be potentially calamitous.

It sounds almost trite to even mention it. However, there have been occasions where errors such as missing zeros in dollar amounts were not detected when supposedly checked. Imagine the consequences of omitting a single "zero" from a $10 million contract. It has happened!

Sometimes, the most rigorous check a major contract receives before execution is the verification of page numbering.

It is important to understand some relevant aspects of the nature of human frailty when considering this topic, or any other topic concerning negotiation:

1) We dislike doing uninteresting things (proofreading rates very highly on the uninteresting scale). It fatigues us.

2) When we are fatigued, we are more prone to making errors that we would otherwise not make.

3) Our eyes sometimes see what they think *should* appear on the printed page, rather than what *actually* appears on it.

One final aspect to note about proofreading is that it is the last opportunity — before signature — to capture that crucial amendment you requested that may have been inadvertently (or otherwise) not included in the document. Alternatively, you might just discover a new clause that the other side was "sure they mentioned to you at the last meeting".

Be thorough. Be vigilant. Always.

■ ■ ■

Reviewing the completed agreement in context

A final (and important) step is a complete review of the document in its final form *in the context of the transaction for your organisation*.

For a larger transaction, it is necessary in many organisations to establish a business case for the transaction and to demonstrate the benefits available to the organisation of entering into the deal. This can sometimes be an exhaustive process, as the potential deal is scrutinised by a number of levels of management. The particular organisation's internal criteria are applied to evaluate the levels of risk and return of the proposed deal.

Often, in a protracted contract negotiation, a deal can undergo a number of fundamental changes and variations (eg to fundamental terms such as pricing, timing and risk issues). During the course of the negotiations, the parties become closely involved in negotiating and considering all of these individual aspects.

At the end of the negotiations, the requirement for a further business case evaluation is not always imposed. A deal's risk/return profile may have been considerably altered by variations applied and agreed to during the course of the negotiation.

For example, when evaluating a particular transaction or deal, an organisation might find it acceptable to:

- assume a higher level of risk, in return for charging a higher price;

OR

- it might accept a lower price, in return for assuming a lower level of risk.

However, for it to accept a higher level of risk *and* to also have to charge a lower price, might produce an uneconomic and unacceptable result.

> ## *Golden Rule*
>
> It is possible that two or more types of variation to a contract — when *assessed individually* — might be acceptable to an organisation.
>
> However, *when combined*, they may produce an unacceptable result.

What is often required, therefore, is for someone to critically evaluate the proposed deal *in its finalised form* (taking into account all variations agreed upon during the course of the negotiations), to ascertain whether the transaction is still a worthwhile one for the organisation.

That is, to ensure that the deal still manages to satisfy all relevant internal evaluation criteria.

Chapter 11

CONTRACT DRAFTING PITFALLS

■ ■ ■

Drafting contracts is easy.

Whereas, drafting contracts that will withstand the test of litigation — or are clear enough to actually avoid it — is very, very difficult.

This assumes particular importance if your side in a transaction is the one drafting the contract. This is because courts in most jurisdictions tend to operate on the rule that *any ambiguity will be construed **against** the party drafting the contract.*

If you are the party which drafted a provision capable of more than one interpretation, you are placed in an awkward position when trying to assert *your* interpretation over any other; a judge may be entitled to reject your argument by saying: *If that is what you really meant, you would have actually said it that way in the first place!*

It may indeed sound trite, but it bears repeating: *say what you want and say it clearly*.

Let us now examine a number of pitfalls and difficulties that frequently arise. Some of the issues relate to particular *expressions* commonly used in speech or other areas, where precision is not a paramount requirement. It is often an instinctive process to translate the way we speak into our writing.

Other issues relate to sensible *practices* worthy of your consideration. Some of these can strongly influence the apportionment of (or sometimes, the complete exoneration of a party from) liability. A badly-worded indemnity or consequential loss clause is sufficiently powerful to "turn around" an otherwise "good" contract into one that is unprofitable, unworkable or even a financial disaster.

Many of the difficulties they can cause are avoidable, firstly, by awareness and, secondly, by the exercise of care. A little extra time taken to weed these expressions out and adopting some of the practices, will repay dividends many times over.

Eventually, such best-practice approaches should become second nature for you.

■ ■ ■

Indefinite words

There is a h-u-g-e difference between an archaeologist's concept of what is a reasonable period of time, compared to that of a 100-metre sprint athlete. One is used to dealing in thousands of years and the other is used to dealing in hundredths of a second. The archaeologist might therefore think that a period of one year is a reasonable time. The athlete might think the same way about an hour.

Words such as *reasonable*, *substantial* and *minimal* are often used in contracts to express measures of time and quantity.

It must be understood that these terms are entirely subjective and mean different things to different people.

A fair question when confronted with either term is:

Relative to what?

Answers will differ depending upon the person answering them.

A "substantial" amount of money to someone poor might be $1000. Whereas, a billionaire might only regard $90 million as being "substantial".

One would expect that a "substantial price increase" in a contract will carry a different meaning for a large multinational corporation than it would for a small privately held company. Words such as these cannot be used as objective measures or reference points.

The point is that words such as these are not conducive to certainty. A common theme you will find recurring in the *Commercial Contract for Managers Series* is the following:

> **Uncertainty is the enemy of the businessperson.**

A properly drawn contract defines and clarifies issues. So when you next see wording in a clause of a contract, which states:

> **Cash** *grants* **Carrie** <u>*a reasonable period of time*</u> *to remedy any defect brought to her attention.*

You might consider changing this to a more definitive time period such as:

> **Cash** *grants* **Carrie** <u>*seven days*</u> *to remedy any defect brought to her attention.*

If it is not possible to state a fixed period of time, even a qualification to the word "reasonable" can be of assistance in interpreting the word. For example:

> *Cash* grants *Carrie* *a reasonable period of time* <u>*having regard to the nature of such defect*</u> *to remedy any defect brought to its attention.*

So if the defect were a minor one, the period of time required would be shorter than if the defect were a major one.

It is useful to keep this principle in mind, both during the negotiations and when the time comes to actually draw up the contract.

Anything you can do at the negotiation and drafting stages to narrow (or preferably close) any uncertainty gaps, will prove profitable in avoiding disputes in the future.

Golden Rule

Uncertainty spurs parties onto having their lawyers find and exploit loopholes.

Uncertainty encourages litigation.

Be on the lookout for vague, uncertain and ambiguous words in contracts.

And, when you find them, negotiate changes to them.

■■■

Implied terms

Implied terms do not appear in an agreement as do *express* terms. However, their existence and effect in particular circumstances must be understood in any commercial contract negotiation.

Implied terms can arise in the following circumstances:

- **To give business efficacy to the contract**

  It becomes necessary for a court to imply terms into a contract when the parties fail to incorporate terms to cover a particular situation. When a court does so, it must imply appropriate terms that accord with the presumed intentions of the parties.

  This principle of *business efficacy* was first laid down in an 1889 case in the United Kingdom — where it remains an accepted part of many common law jurisdictions.

  Any term *implied* into a contract by the court must be:

  1) reasonable and equitable;
  2) necessary — without which the contract would be ineffective;
  3) so obvious that it "goes without saying";
  4) capable of clear expression; and
  5) must not contradict any express term of the contract.

- **Because of a custom or trade usage**

  This arises where one or both of the parties are engaged in a particular industry or trade. In such a case, the customs or usages of that industry or trade may be implied into the contract.

- **Terms implied by statute**

  Numerous statutes imply terms into contracts. Usually such statutes make it illegal to attempt to contract out of or attempt to exclude any rights created by the statute.

  In Australia, the most common examples are the *Sale of Goods Act* and the *Trade Practices Act*, which imply terms as to quality and fitness for purpose into certain contracts for the sale of goods.

- **Terms implied through a *course of dealing* between the parties**

  A court, in attempting to interpret the parties' intentions may have regard to the past dealings of the parties. A court may imply terms into a contract under this category, by considering:

  1) the length of time over which dealings had been conducted; and
  2) the consistency of the previous conduct that the court is being asked to imply into the current agreement.

  It is important to realise that, under some circumstances, conduct by the parties (inconsistent with, or different to, the written terms of the contract), can have the effect of actually amending the contract.

■ ■ ■

Extra or unnecessary wording

The more words you use to express a simple intention, the more potential ambiguity you risk creating. This may then make it possible for the other party to ask the court to favour its interpretation over yours.

Any court looking at your contract should be able to establish all of the terms of the deal from just reading the contract (and not having to look at anything else or hear from anyone else). The court should also be able to gain an understanding of the parties' intentions of what they wished the document to achieve.

If you do not clearly express what you require in a contract document, you run the risk of a court implying terms into the agreement that may well be contrary to your original intentions.

As you have seen in the section above, courts have the power to imply a term into the contract where the circumstances warrant. Courts will generally ask *whether the parties would have agreed to it*. An investigation into the parties' presumed intention is a necessary part of this process. The test is *not* whether it would have been reasonable for them to do so.

You have a greater power at your disposal to avoid the intervention of a court: clear and unambiguous drafting.

Another important rule applies here; economy of words. Do not be tempted to say in 50 words what can be better said in ten.

A frequent argument with those prone to verbose contract drafting is their proposition that the extra words "don't have any effect" or "don't change the interpretation". However, there is always a chance that they *might*.

Even assuming they do not, there is no place for redundant wording. More often than not, such extra and unnecessary wording is contained in a precedent document retrieved "off the shelf". Laziness in redrafting or tailoring such a precedent document can often account for the excess verbiage.

One final point to note: people who have a tendency to talk interminably and make extravagant claims during the negotiation, can sometimes translate that tendency into contract drafting that "breaks the rules" — the contract may contain redundant, ambiguous or unnecessary terms.

■ ■ ■

"Plain English" or "legalese"?

As with most forms of legal documents, contracts can take the form of either the newer style "plain English" documents or the more traditional "legalese" ones using archaic and unfamiliar (to the non-lawyer) language and expression.

In traditional drafting, one must only consider the legal effect of the words used. Ease of reading is a distinctly secondary consideration. This is why it is common to see long unbroken paragraphs without so much as a comma separating the text. Some sections often have to be read more than once to be properly understood.

On the other hand, in plain English drafting (by its very definition), ease of reading also becomes a primary objective. With both considerations in mind, drafting can become an arduous task.

For the moment, it seems that "legalese" tends to dominate drafting styles, since many lawyers tend to be comfortable and familiar with what they often justify as "tried and tested" phrases in documents.

However, it is useful to bear in mind, as a general point, that the more unnecessary words used in a particular expression, the greater the potential for a misunderstanding or a loophole to be lurking.

To illustrate the point, consider a sign along the following lines:

> *This machine has numerous moving parts that could snare or otherwise catch any loose article of clothing, ties, long hair, hands or fingers. In such event, you could become trapped by the machine and could thereby sustain severe or life-threatening injuries such as loss of a limb (or partial loss thereof) or even asphyxiation. Therefore, it is highly recommended — in the strongest possible terms — that you keep well away from the machine and also keep others away, to prevent the possibility of such injuries or death from occurring.*

Complicated isn't it? On its face, it appears exhaustive and thorough. However, by the time you were close enough to read and understand the message, your proximity to the machine greatly increases your chances of actually suffering the same injuries that the sign is attempting to warn you against. The more unnecessary words used, the greater the possibility for errors arising.

Consider the effect of the same sign using simplified and more direct language, leaving little room for error or misinterpretation:

DANGER — KEEP CLEAR

Which do you find more direct and effective?

Golden Rule

The greatest control over implied terms is achieved by carefully drafting express terms to be as clear and unambiguous as possible.

Then, expressly disclaim all else.

■■■

Meaning of "in consultation with"

The appearance of the words "in consultation with" is usually a consequence of poor drafting and lack of forethought.

It can often appear as a clause along the following lines:

Yin must consult with Yang prior to [taking a certain specified action].

Each party usually has a different interpretation and understanding of the meaning of the expression "consult with":

1) **Yin** could consider it to mean that he merely has to notify **Yang** that he intends taking such action.

   "Notify" meaning, "tell", not "ask"!

He would then consider himself to be at liberty to pursue such action without hindrance or obstruction from **Yang**.

2) Conversely, **Yang** may consider it to mean that **Yin** cannot take such action *until* he obtains the consent of **Yang**.

The inference being that **Yang** has some say or influence over whether the action actually takes place.

The first interpretation is generally the favoured one. Many lawyers would hold the view (one also shared by many judges) that if **Yang** was supposed to first give his consent to **Yin** to allow him to take action, then the contract would have, expressly and unambiguously, said so!

However, the point is that the use of wording such as "in consultation with" creates uncertainty and the potential for misunderstanding between the parties.

A properly drawn contract is supposed to clarify and clearly define issues between parties.

*It should **settle** issues rather than **create** them.*

Case study: confusion between countries (not just companies)

"In consultation with"

In the early 1990s, the United States government decided to return control of the archives of the remaining Third Reich personnel records to Germany.

The agreement reached provided that in the event that files were to be moved to other regional archives, the relevant German authorities were required to *consult* with US authorities before moving the collection.

However, the German authorities interpreted *consult* to mean that Germany was only required to *inform* the US of its intentions to move the relevant documents.

It did not consider the use of the word *consult* to mean that permission or consent was required from the US.

The ensuing controversy could have been avoided by careful initial thought. This was simply a case of the Americans' drafting of the agreement failing to express what they actually wanted (ie, the precise steps that had to be taken), in the event of relocation of the archives.

> ### Golden Rule
>
> Ambiguity in contracts is the enemy of the businessperson.
>
> Always choose expressions and words that are clear and unambiguous.

■ ■ ■

Giving authority to accept verbal instructions

When it comes to giving important directions concerning a written contract, the best way is to do it in writing.

For example, consider a fictitious agreement for a corporate motor fleet. An important part of this agreement was the procedure to be followed for the:

- addition of newly acquired vehicles to the fleet; and

- disposal or retirement of vehicles from the fleet.

This agreement contained a term that enabled the fleet company to act on verbal instructions to acquire new vehicles for the corporate fleet.

You would want to be reasonably certain that if the fleet company received a telephone call committing your company to an order of 100 pink Porsches, that it should require formal written notification from an appropriately authorised officer of your company — *before* being authorised to act on such an order and proceeding to purchase the vehicles for your company.

Presumably, your company wouldn't authorise and empower *any* employee to make such multi-million dollar capital purchases, by telephone, without first obtaining other appropriate internal approvals.

However, a requirement for written authorisation may not always appear as it seems.

Take the following clause from the same corporate motor vehicle fleet leasing agreement described above. This clause was buried deep within a multi-page agreement as one of several sub-clauses (not at all easy to detect, on a cursory glance).

The Lessee shall indemnify to the extent permitted by any applicable law, and keep indemnified, the Fleet Provider from and against all loss, damages, claims and expenses suffered or incurred by the Fleet Provider resulting directly or indirectly from any breach by the Lessee of any of its obligations hereunder or from the Fleet Provider acting in good faith on any Vehicle Order or other instructions (whether transmitted by telephone, facsimile, telex or otherwise) purporting to originate from the Lessee's offices or to have been given by an authorised officer of the Lessee.

Let us carefully examine the effect of the above clause by highlighting some key aspects:

1) The clause provides that the Lessee (the company leasing the vehicles) agrees to cover any loss suffered by the Fleet Provider (the leasing company) where it acted "in good faith" on *any* vehicle order or instructions, *including those received by telephone.*

2) Assume the janitor has placed a telephone order with the Fleet Provider for 100 pink Porsches for immediate delivery.

3) The Fleet Provider is required to be able to demonstrate that the instructions *appeared* to have come from the Lessee company *or* from an authorised officer. Therefore, the clause effectively gives the leasing company the authority to act on telephone orders for new vehicles as long as such orders *purport* to originate from the Lessee's offices! Of course, our janitor easily satisfies that requirement by saying, *I'm calling from the Lessee company.*

Important notices such as capital expenditure authorisations, termination notices and the like, should always be required to be given in writing to minimise the possibility or likelihood of confusion or misunderstandings arising as to what was actually said and by whom.

Golden Nugget

Did you notice?

In any contract, important notices such as termination notices or dispute notices, should be restricted to being able to be **given by** *and* **addressed to** a restricted category of person, of a suitably senior rank. For example, "The Company Secretary", the "Chief Executive Officer", etc.

In the **"Service of Notices"** provision in the contract, it is best to use the relevant person's title, rather than their name. Otherwise, you risk creating confusion, if that person has changed or left their position, during the course of the contract. For example, an important notice comes through the fax for the attention of Mr Smith. An office junior, who knows Mr Smith has left the company the week before, might, upon seeing the fax, mistakenly discard it.

In that way, you avoid the risk of damaging a commercial relationship through a misunderstanding causing a dispute as to whether one million or ten million widgets were ordered or whether they were required for delivery on the 24th of the month and not on the 29th.

If there are a number of repetitive actions of such importance likely during the course of a contract, the best way is to agree on the layout and contents of a standard form that can be used for the purpose. Ideally, such a form would be referred to within the contract and a copy would form part of the contract in a schedule attached to the contract.

When the particular notice is required to be given, all that would then be needed would be for the appropriate blanks to be completed, the form signed by the authorised officer and faxed.

A lasting and (usually) unequivocal record would then remain documenting the action and its timing.

Golden Rule

Verbal instructions are not worth the paper they're (not) written on.

Always choose to document important actions under a contract, in writing.

■ ■ ■

"Best endeavours" or "best efforts"

The words "best endeavours" or "best efforts" usually attach to a general obligation. For example, a party to a contract may be required to perform its obligations using *best endeavours.*

There are subtle differences on the meaning and force of the phrase depending upon the particular jurisdiction.

It is also important to consider whether you are seeking another party to perform a best endeavours obligation or whether you are being called upon to give it.

Recognise firstly, that it is an uncertain and vague standard. There are even cases of courts ruling the phrase to be so vague as to be unenforceable.

In understanding the meaning of "best endeavours", our starting point is the highest standard; the highest standard achievable is a positive unqualified obligation.

An example would be:

R Chu shall sell 100 units per day.

This is a positive and unqualified obligation. **R Chu** *must* sell 100 units per day, "no matter what". As there are no qualifications to the obligation, compliance is mandatory. Any non-compliance with the requirement, for any reason, would immediately place **R Chu** in breach of contract.

The positive obligation above imposes a far higher duty on **R Chu** than a clause which provides that:

> *R Chu shall use his **reasonable endeavours** to sell 100 units per day.*

This clause gives **R Chu** sufficient "room" to be able to demonstrate why he was not able to comply with the target quantity. Factors such as a depressed market or any other valid reason might provide **R Chu** with a successful defence to any action of breach of contract.

The notion of "best endeavours" was traditionally viewed by many as the "next best thing" to a positive obligation. In jurisdictions such as Australia, it probably is the next best thing. In other jurisdictions such as the USA and the UK, it is not.

The obligation includes taking such action which is commercially practicable. There is no requirement for an organisation to "spend itself into bankruptcy". The duty is almost certainly something equal to, if not more than, "good faith efforts".

In most jurisdictions a "best endeavours" duty includes a duty to "act in good faith" or to "act reasonably". However, the converse is *not* usually true. A duty to act in good faith does *not* usually include an obligation to use best endeavours.

While the element of reasonableness forms an integral part of a "best endeavours" obligation, an obligation to use "reasonable endeavours" or "reasonable efforts" is an even lesser duty. It has been described as "appreciably less than 'best endeavours'".

In the UK, courts have held that the phrase *all reasonable endeavours* is the middle position between "best endeavours" and "reasonable endeavours".

Therefore, if you are depending on an absolute level of performance from the other party to a contract, you can rest assured that a requirement for that other party to use its "reasonable endeavours" to perform those obligations, will **not** give you the comfort or legal protection in the event that they fail to do so.

The best way to achieve proper and more certain legal protection is to specify specific positive obligations, by reference to what the term actually means to you, in the context of the outcomes you require in that particular deal.

Contracts offer far more certainty when their drafting is outcome-driven.

Golden Rule

If you are asked to perform using "best endeavours", try to negotiate down to at least "reasonable endeavours".

If you are on the other side wanting to secure a "best endeavours" level of performance from the other party, the ideal way to avoid any ambiguity is to actually specify the steps you want the other party to take in order to achieve the end result you require.

Negotiating indemnity clauses

An indemnity is a contractual commitment by a party to make good a specified loss suffered by the other party. In other words, it is an acknowledgment and promise by one party to cover the potential liability of another.

The reason why indemnity clauses are one of the primary pitfalls in any contract, is that the repercussions of indemnities "gone wrong" can be enormous.

Indemnities are an important and complex area of contracts. The extent of the problems created by indemnities tends to be magnified when grappling with the issue of consequential loss and damage.

A key feature of an indemnity is that the obligation created by it can often extend *beyond* that which would otherwise be imposed on a party under the general law. For that reason, they should be given sparingly.

The very concept of an indemnity is to make the injured party whole again, as if the loss had not occurred, even if the person who agrees to indemnify would not otherwise have had any obligation to do so.

Indemnities are not always simply black–or–white issues. The issue is not always confined to: *Do I provide an indemnity or not?*

Indemnities can be qualified by certain exceptions and exclusions. With careful evaluation, subtle changes can often create significant effects in reducing or minimising liability. You should exercise great caution here, as the converse can also apply.

This can become a veritable minefield for the inexperienced.

Every executive reading or signing contracts needs to have a basic understanding of indemnities and their, potentially, far-reaching effects.

Checklist: reasons why indemnity clauses may be deficient

There are generally five main reasons why indemnity clauses are deficient:

1) Liability extends well beyond the terms of the contract or even for negligence alone.

2) There is no exception for the negligent acts or omissions of third parties not under the direct control of the party giving the indemnity.

3) There is no exception for the negligence, acts or omissions of the other party to the contract.

4) There is no reduction in liability *to the extent* of negligence.

5) There is no specific and express exclusion for consequential or indirect loss or damage.

The rule-of-thumb "plain English" principle to be generally applied in indemnities, is:

- if we mess up, we are responsible for the direct consequences;

- if you mess up, you are responsible for the direct consequences;

- if someone under our control is to blame, we are responsible;

- if we share the blame, then we share responsibility to the extent that we are each to blame; and

- if someone other than someone under our control is to blame, we are not responsible.

In considering *any* indemnity provision, it is important to pay close attention to the *substance* of the party with whom you are contracting. Having a clause to "protect" you is not sufficient if the other party has no means to satisfy any potential future claim.

■ ■ ■

Consequential loss provisions

Consequential loss provisions extend the (already potentially problematic) liability created by indemnities, even further.

Since they have the potential to bankrupt a large company (in an extreme case), they are of enormous significance and importance.

It can be argued that consequential loss clauses are not normal or reasonable commercial terms.

- *normal* or *direct* loss is that which flows directly from a breach of contract or other action;

- consequential loss is the loss suffered because of the *circumstances peculiar to a particular person or entity*. It can often be referred to as an *indirect* loss.

By their very nature, consequential losses are uncertain and difficult to quantify.

The argument against the use of a consequential loss clause is that it allows the category of damages that can be claimed, to be *unfairly broadened* and *extends liability beyond the normal commercial realm*.

Consequential loss clauses involve the acceptance of responsibility for risks that are not foreseeable and not within the ordinary knowledge of the party being required to provide such protection. Indeed, in some circumstances, the risks can even extend to include the losses of persons who are not parties to the agreement!

However, in a situation where you are compelled to accept a consequential loss provision in an agreement, two methods of reducing exposure under a consequential loss provision are:

1) **Restrict the ambit of the clause**

    Where a party has specific concerns relating to a *particular* event/s of consequential loss, then the category of consequential loss should be specifically limited only to such an event/s.

2) **Impose a ceiling or "cap" on the maximum liability under such a clause**

    For example, the maximum liability under the clause could be expressed to be the purchase price paid under the agreement.

To develop a better understanding and to view a more comprehensive treatment of indemnity clauses and consequential losses, with examples of their use, you should consult **Understanding Indemnity Clauses**, the first volume in the *Commercial Contracts for Managers Series*.

Chapter 12

RULES OF CONTRACT INTERPRETATION

■ ■ ■

Legal rules to consider at the "front end"

Legal rules of contract interpretation are important to bear in mind at the *front end* of the contract process; that is, when recording the deal points, as and when, you agree to them, during a negotiation.

The following rules should be considered *during* contract negotiations, as they will help you prevent contract problems from occurring. Having to address such problems after they arise, is invariably more complex, time-consuming and expensive.

In addition, front-end solutions help to preserve valuable goodwill and hard-won commercial relationships, rather than relying on reactive solutions, devised after the event, to attempt to salvage the remains of (by then, often hostile) relationships.

■ ■ ■

Requirement that an agreement be in writing

Some categories of contracts are required to be in writing.

The English *Act for the Prevention of Frauds and Perjuries*, enacted in 1677, called the Statute of Frauds, aimed to ensure that contracts for important matters were required to be *in writing* and signed by the parties. The purpose of the statute — as its name suggests — was to prevent fraud.

A reference to the term, Statute of Frauds, is now taken to mean any law that requires certain contracts to be in writing and signed by the parties.

The concept has since been adopted in the laws of virtually every English-speaking jurisdiction and many non-English-speaking ones.

The most common types of contracts to which the statute applies are contracts that involve the sale or transfer of land and contracts of guarantee (for example, where Harley guarantees the payment of a debt owed by Davidson, to a dealer, for the purchase of a motorcycle). The effect is that, in many jurisdictions, agreements for the sale of land or contracts of guarantee are not valid unless they are in writing.

Different jurisdictions will individually define the extent of coverage of their own Statute of Frauds. Some will extend to include areas of the sale of goods and consumer credit transactions.

In Australia, the Statute of Frauds was inherited as part of the local law by each colony at the time of settlement. It remains in force (in a modified form) in some states. In other states, the Statute has been abolished, although the concept has been incorporated into other laws. For example, in New South Wales, the requirement for an agreement for the sale of land to be in writing is now contained in the *Conveyancing Act*.

The concept behind the Statute of Frauds may well become relevant in the future, as an increasing number of transactions are conducted, not in person, but electronically.

Electronic transactions legislation that has, or will, be enacted in many jurisdictions, will duly consider the Statute of Frauds concept — in a more modern context — but with the same ends in mind.

■■■

Use of extrinsic evidence

The *parol evidence* rule is not to be confused with the Statute of Frauds. The purpose and scope of this rule is different. The object of the Statute of Frauds was to prevent false (perjured) testimony being offered, during court proceedings, to prove the existence of *certain types of contracts*. The parol evidence rule differs in that it applies to *any* contract.

The rule is that extrinsic evidence cannot be used to interpret the terms of the contract. As with many rules in law, it contains a number of exceptions: one of which is that extrinsic evidence may be admitted to clear up an ambiguity.

One might be tempted to ask, *How is this rule relevant to commercial contract negotiations?*

The reason the rule is discussed in this book is to highlight the fact that, in litigation, *evidence of prior negotiations may be allowed to establish objectively what the parties intended.* However, the exception to the rule cannot be used for a party to simply say, *this is what I meant* in relation to a particular clause in a document.

This is yet another reason why concise and accurate note taking (or recording of minutes) during a negotiation is an important step, which can pay dividends in the long run.

Golden Rule

When you are negotiating, realise that what the parties *say*, may later be relevant and admissible in a court.

That is, what is said in negotiations may later be used to establish objective facts, which may be used to interpret the intention of the parties.

The purpose of the rule is to ensure that the understanding of the parties — as embodied within a written agreement — is not altered, except by another agreement in writing.

A useful tool to reinforce the operation of the rule is the use of an *entire agreement clause*. This is a clause to the effect that the entire agreement between the parties is contained within the written document. Such a clause might look like this:

This Agreement contains the entire terms of the agreement and understanding between the parties. Each of the parties acknowledge that in entering into this Agreement on the terms set out in this Agreement it is not relying upon any representation, warranty, promise or assurance made or given by any other party or any other person, whether or not in writing, at any time prior to the execution of this Agreement which is not expressly set out in this Agreement.

■ ■ ■

Ambiguity in contract clauses

The *contra proferentem* rule states that any ambiguity in contract clauses will be interpreted against the interests of the party that drafted the agreement.

So that if a party makes an error in contract wording and fails to extend an exclusion clause to exclude a particular set of circumstances, it must meet any claim made which is not expressly excluded.

For example: an exclusion of "implied warranties", in a contract, will not be effective in excluding liability for:

- *express* warranties; or even
- implied *conditions*.

In the same way, any exclusion of *consequential loss* will not be effective in excluding liability for *direct loss*.

Golden Nugget

Say what you really mean

The following example serves as an illustration of the lengths that a court may go to, in order to construe ambiguous contract provisions against the party that drafted them.

In a 1924 case, decided in England, the disclaimer in a particular contract provided that any claim by the purchaser in respect of "goods delivered" had to be made "within 14 days". The actual clause read, in part:

> *The goods delivered shall be deemed to be in all respects in accordance with the contract... unless the sellers shall within 14 days after the arrival of the goods receive notice...*

The purchaser made a claim against the seller some 18 months later, complaining that some of the goods, that were supposed to have been supplied, had been short-delivered.

In applying the *contra proferentem* rule, the court held that the exclusion clause did *not* apply as it was only concerned with "goods delivered" and the purchaser's claim was in respect of goods that had *not* been delivered.

Golden Rule

It is important to always keep this rule (together with the parol evidence rule) in mind at all stages of the negotiation, when considering the drafting of the final contract documenting the transaction.

This applies more particularly so, if you are the party having control of the drafting of the contract documentation.

Chapter 13

CONCLUSION

■■■

Happy endings — another satisfied customer

It is greatly satisfying to have developed a mutually acceptable resolution of a problem by overcoming — what were originally thought to be — insurmountable negotiating obstacles, along the way.

Sometimes, when the parties are too far apart on one or more fundamental issues, a deal cannot be achieved. If the parties must walk away from one another, it is best that it occurs due to the irreconcilable positions of the parties rather than the stubbornness or intractability of one of them. The door is then left open for the parties to do business in the future.

It is rare for a negotiation to break down on only one point, before alternative options are considered. In many situations, there will almost certainly be alternative choices and other ways of achieving a result available. Often, they will not be readily apparent.

Creativity and lateral thinking are the keys to avoiding the "this is our only option" trap.

Negotiations do not need to be trench warfare battles, in which every minor point conceded is to be taken as a personal affront.

Indeed, the most experienced negotiators are genuinely interested in helping the other party get what they want out of the negotiation. This is not because of any special "touchy feely" reason, but simply because it makes good business sense to help another party explore different ways that it might achieve its particular objectives, without necessarily compromising or interfering with your own.

Just because one party wins, it does not necessarily mean that the other loses.

Such an interest in the other party's needs and of the *why* behind those needs, fosters the development of a relationship in which the credibility of a party can be depended upon to help develop collaborative and mutually satisfactory solutions to negotiating problems.

That is not to say experienced negotiators do not fight; they most certainly do.

However, the difference is that they choose their battles carefully and know when to invest time and effort into achieving the points that really matter to them. Along the way, they can concede non-material points to maintain the momentum of the negotiation proceedings.

A lot of what makes a person a good negotiator are people skills, listening skills and common sense. Being able to read people and size-up a situation can make an enormous difference. Reacting well under the pressures of a negotiation (particularly when the stakes are high) is something that cannot be easily taught; it must be experienced.

Hopefully, this book has taught you a number of things to do (and some things to avoid or watch out for) to help smooth the transition of the negotiated bargain into a contract document that the parties are willing to sign and abide by.

If you recognise a ploy or gambit being used against you in your next negotiation, and know how to react to counter it, then this book will have achieved its objective.

Finally, it pays to remember that negotiations do not end when you have reached agreement to a deal, as the level of scrutiny and vigilance required at the contract stage is of equal importance. This crucial fact can sometimes be overlooked in the euphoria and relief at having finally struck a deal.

Remember, the purpose of negotiation is to strike a mutually acceptable and workable deal.

An important part of finalising this process is to ensure that the agreement reached is properly translated into a clear and unambiguous contract document — with such document being an accurate reflection of the parties' intention and understanding of the transaction.

Golden Nugget

Make your lawyer your friend, not your enemy

Some managers may be tempted to regard lawyers (perhaps unfairly) in the same manner as Mario Puzo's character Don Corleone, in the *Godfather*, who observed:

> *A lawyer with a briefcase can steal more than a thousand men with guns.*

Some managers may take the view that lawyers have a desire to either complicate things, or to insist on negotiating every minute point "to the death".

Happily, this is not the philosophy of a vast majority of commercial lawyers.

In the event that the disasters warned of or predicted by a lawyer, do not eventuate, this should be music to the ears of lawyers and managers alike. It is indeed confirmation that the lawyers and managers have both performed their respective tasks correctly.

What must be appreciated, is that the seemingly endless discussions spent "hammering out", what may have seemed "minute points", often contributes significantly to clarifying the understanding and intentions of the parties.

Venting all of the competing views *before* signing the contract is conducive to reaching an agreement and achieving common ground.

Attempting to do so *afterwards,* can sometimes be conducive to souring commercial relationships and may lead to litigation.

Golden Rule

In business, a contract that is properly and carefully negotiated and drawn up, is less likely to *need* to be referred to by the parties, during the life of the contract.

A contract document tends to be rarely, if ever, consulted by the parties until there is a dispute. At such time, the contract document is one of the first things that the lawyers will ask to see.

The parting message of the book is to be aware of matters but to not take caution to extremes.

Case study: taking caution to extremes

Leading Australian barrister, Ian Barker, QC, once wrote about a stairway at the Downing Centre court complex in Sydney, which had been closed for several years. He wrote:

The amazing closed stairway remains closed. A sign tells the reader it is closed pending a "compliance check".

It is obviously a very thorough check; as the stairway has been closed for some three years. In fact, the stairway was closed in an excess of bureaucratic timidity because someone fell and sued the State.

I am glad that whoever made the decision is not running the State's transport system.

This is, obviously, taking caution to extremes.

There is always risk in business.

Aim to strike a balance by being sensible and taking calculated risks.

The key is to ensure that you precisely *identify* and *understand* the risks. Only then, are you are in a position to make a commercial judgment on whether to accept or reject a deal (based — among other things — upon the likely return it will generate).

Let us close with a light-hearted look at the ten "golden rules" of negotiation.

It is my sincere hope that you will not find these "rules" bearing any resemblance to current corporate conduct or work practices in any company you work for or know of.

Ten golden rules of negotiation

THE RULES

1 The company has enjoyed success in its major commercial negotiations over the years, and has developed considerable expertise from which it has distilled these rules for the benefit of managers involved in commercial negotiations.

Do the deal, at all costs. The chief executive will already have told the board that it will be done, so it must. In practical terms, for the company's negotiators the translation is simple — give away the farm, at the earliest opportunity. This is the paramount rule, against which all others are subordinate.

2 Open the kimono as early as possible in negotiations. Sharing our bottom-line with the other side helps demonstrate our genuineness. Never, ever try to find the other party's bottom-line. It would be idle speculation to do so, yet we know precisely where ours is — it should remain our guiding light at all times. If inadvertently we *do* identify the other side's bottom-line, and they become disillusioned or disengage from negotiations, admonish our team's failure. Offer the other side whatever it takes to get them back to a comfortable place, preferably well above their last position.

3 Disregard misguided suggestions to prepare a coordinated negotiation strategy in advance. The other side can always be relied on to set the agenda, and to provide the framework for constructive negotiations in accordance with the paramount goal of Rule One.

4 If any member of the team breaks Rule Three, any such negotiation strategy should be rejected and disregarded — especially if all members of the core negotiating team have endorsed it. Great care should be taken to act in accordance with these rules rather than any such pre-prepared strategy.

5 Executive management must never be seen to support the negotiating team. Negotiators thrive on challenge, and welcome the opportunity to spend more time focussed internally than against the other side. The negotiation team especially welcomes if, without consulting them, senior management gives away any position they are trying to maintain.

6 Teamwork is an overrated management fad. Any signs of the advancement of a sense of cohesive purpose by the negotiating team almost inevitably runs counter to the spirit of these rules, and should actively be dissuaded.

7 If the other side even so much as hints that anyone on our team might prove an effective block to full farm transfer, any request to remove or marginalise that person should immediately be met. Such people are cancerous growths who risk infecting other team members. They should be cut out as soon as the other side usefully helps us identify them.

8 Before any deal is actually struck, always advise the board, and the market, of the terms of the deal. This usefully gives the other side an opportunity to seek any part of the farm we may inadvertently have retained, as the final price for consummating the deal we say we've already done. Elaborate publicly announced plans for a joint press conference, international travel underway by the most senior managers on both sides, and a joint press release are all useful tools for driving further concessions the other side might genuinely require.

9 The contribution of those most actively involved in negotiations should generally be minimised, especially if negotiations resulted in the retention of large parts of the farm in breach of Rule One. Good management practice also requires that those not directly involved in core negotiations — especially those who would sensibly follow these rules without irritating questions — should be recognised, rewarded and promoted.

10 After the contract is signed, it should neither be retained nor subsequently referred to — especially by operational managers responsible for its implementation. It may, however, be appropriate immediately to instruct the company's lawyers to investigate how best to avoid any binding commitments inadvertently contained in the contract.

Finally, these rules must be closely followed, yet should never be expressed or revealed. They are unique, and represent a fundamental cornerstone of the company's competitive advantage.

First published in Lawyers Weekly *magazine and reproduced with the kind permission of the author.*

INDEX

OTHER TITLES IN THE SERIES

Before you sign a contract understand its essential elements. There are also tip and hints about the many pitfalls and advice on avoiding future disputes.

ISBN: 978-085297-773-6   224 pages

Particular contract clauses (boilerplate clauses) are important in commercial contracts. Some executives will only scrutinise the commercial or "deal" terms of the contract. The rest is usually left for the lawyers. However, the boilerplate clause will usually govern or regulate the other clauses. They are vital.

ISBN: 978-0-85297-758-3   192 pages

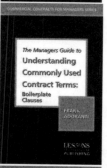

This book explains the essential elements necessary for a complete confidentiality agreement. You will learn how unscrupulous players use confidentiality agreements to gain an unfair advantage, and how to avoid getting "caught".

ISBN: 978-0-85297-757-6   116 pages

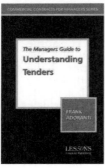